"Flip the Script is such a powerful book! Dr. Cooper provides a simple, impactful plan to create powerful changes in your results and life. It challenges and inspires! It has motivated me and gave me a clear direction to continue to reach my true and real potential!"

—**Kevin Jackson**, Olympic Champion,
Former United State National Team Coach

"Dr. Cooper's book provides a practical process to implement powerful daily habits in your life, that in turn "Flip the Script" on your most common barriers, so you can reach your highest potential. These practices have given me the expanded ability and energy to lead and live my life to the fullest."

—**Laurie Gere**, Mayor of Anacortes,
Founder/Owner of Gere-a-Deli, Entrepreneur/Business Leader

"Coyte Cooper is one of my all-time favorite people on the planet! For a couple of reasons. First, he is the real deal as he does not give advice that he doesn't already live by. Second, he always challenges my thinking and approach. This book is no exception. It will continue to be a resource that I keep very close and reference often. I think you will feel the same after reading Flip the Script. Coyte will help you see a better future and give you the tools to create it."

—**Ken Hubbard**, Pastor at Radius Church,
Author, Leadership Expert

"Success is something you must pursue if you want to bring it to fruition. Dr. Cooper has the expertise to outline the specific steps you can take that will help you create habits that allow you to achieve your highest aspirations."

—**Cindy Miller**, Former LPGA Player, Speaker,
Coach and Corporate Trainer

"Dr. Cooper's burning desire to win and uncanny level of discipline has launched him into his destiny as a full-time author, life coach, and speaker. He will be known as one of the top motivators among people who want to achieve greatness and make their mark in this world!"

—**Josh Liske**, President of IHP Global,
Divisional Supervisor at Midwest Division, Author of Up Yours.

"Having had the opportunity to meet Coyte in person and attend his seminar, it's refreshing to see he practices what he preaches. Demonstrating a true passion for small but mighty changes, this book will leave you motivated and excited to live your best life. A must read!"

—**Heather Altepeter,** Founder and CEO of
National Merchants Association (billion dollar company), Author, Investor

"I never realized how much more potential I had until I started to work with Dr. Coyte Cooper. He helps you realize that the path to your dreams is not easy, but with consistent daily effort, we can earn the right to success."

—**Derek Moore,** NCAA Champion, Coach and Entrepreneur

"Coyte Cooper has changed my life. He has a profound way of teaching people how to "flip the script" and redirect our minds to focus on the positive and priorities in our life. I have purpose, clarity, and can envision a life by my design now and it was through his training and leadership that I believed in me again."

—**Natalie Rene,** Business Owner and Fitness/Wellness Coach

"Having the opportunity to work with Dr. Cooper has had a tremendous impact on my overall personal and professional growth. He truly understands the importance of building positive relationships that make lasting impressions. He lives each and every day with gratitude, energy, and a sincere excitement for helping others around him, and I've become better in all aspects because of him."

—**Scott Grant,** CEO/Founder of Triple Threat Leadership

"I believe how you think has everything to do with how you perform and what you attain. Flip the Script hits the nail on the head for how you decide to live your life when your world gets turned upside down. One decision will guarantee disappointment and another a challenge to find your highest potential. Just sit back, dig in, turn the page and climb out into the sunshine."

—**Jim Miller,** 10x NCAA Champion and Hall of Fame Coach

"Dr. Coyte Cooper is one of the most influential and relatable voices in personal development today. He has helped more individuals and businesses achieve their desired results than anyone else in the game. Coyte's new book, "Flip the Script" is his best work yet and a strong example of how Coyte's process can take a person or an organization from being an average performer to being the best in their class. This book will show you how to turnaround the negative situations, negative people and negative emotions infecting your life so you can start outmaneuvering and outpacing the competition and finally achieve the level of success you deserve. If you want to get ahead but are not getting the results you want, start by reading "Flip the Script" by Coyte Cooper."

—**Isaiah Hankel,** Bestselling Author, Speaker, Founder/CEO of Cheeky Scientist

FLIP THE SCRIPT

FL!P THE SCRIPT

TRAIN YOUR BRAIN TO BREAKTHROUGH YOUR BIGGEST
BARRIERS & RELEASE YOUR HIGHEST POTENTIAL

COYTE COOPER, PH.D.

Cover and book design by Vincent Vi
Manufactured in the United States of America

For more information, please contact:

Coyte Cooper, Ph.D.
Earn the Right Incorporated
www.coytecooper.com
coytecooper@ollinliving.com

ISBN: 978-0-9905636-4-8

To my wife, Brandy.

*For telling me to "go for it" and never once asking me
to give up on my dream.*

*You have believed in me every step of the way and I will always love you
with all of my heart for that. This entire journey
was only possible because of you.*

THE FLIPPIN
CONTENTS

THE DECISION THAT FLIPPED
MY LIFE UPSIDE DOWN

It was a serene Spring day in Chapel Hill. The flowers were now in full bloom as their vibrant colors complemented the tall pine trees that I loved so much. They reminded me of Washington state, a place where I had grown up and adored even more the farther I moved away from it. I had always admired the fact that the pines delivered some much-needed vibrancy during the otherwise dormant winter months. They also happened to be my favorite part of the football stadium that resided to my right as I arrived on campus. It was surrounded by droves of pines that stretched up hundreds of feet to the top of the 55,000+ seat stadium. It was truly a picturesque scene. Cruising past the stadium, I pulled into a space where I had been parking for the last six years.

As I shut the door on my Toyota Tacoma truck, I patted the hood two times before heading down the stairs towards my boss's office. With the birds singing around me, I couldn't help but dance a little as I made my way down the long brick walkway that had become a staple of the university. These had always made a unique impression on me. I marveled at the fact that there were literally hundreds of thousands of bricks that had been meticulously placed all over campus. I had always imagined them as magical paths created to guide students on their journey to go out and make their mark on the world. When combined with the pristine historic buildings and the immaculate landscaping, you could see why so many people thought the University of North Carolina was such an incredibly special place.

Nearing the end of the walkway, I reminisced about the first time I had ever been on campus. It had been for an interview and despite it being December I had been thoroughly blown away by the beauty of the UNC campus and the energy I felt while on it. There didn't seem to be a single person I met during the grueling two-day interview that did not love being at the university. It seemed like the perfect scenario for the next step in my career. I smiled briefly when remembering how I had returned to the historic hotel at the end of the interview to tell my wife Brandy that this was where we would be living next year. She had smiled and responded, "So, it went that well?"

When offered the position a few months later, I eagerly accepted and we promptly made plans to move to Chapel Hill at the end of the school year. At times, I felt like I had to pinch myself because I had landed my "dream job," one that others in my field would do about anything to have, at the age of 28. I had officially become an Assistant Professor at one of the most prestigious public universities in the United States. The fact that Brandy had always imagined living in North Carolina made it all seem too good to be true. We quickly settled in to the area when building our first house in a beautiful subdivision surrounded by tall pine trees. It was the perfect place for us to start a family. We proceeded to have two gorgeous children, Carter and Mya, and everything felt like home.

Time sure does fly by, I pondered. *It seems like just yesterday that we arrived here in Chapel Hill. It has all gone by in a flash. I blink and Mya is already two and Carter will be in Kindergarten soon. I guess the saying is correct about time flying by when you are having fun.* Just before proceeding to my next thought, I was interrupted by the sound of shuffling feet scurrying in front of me. Glancing up to see the source of the sound, I realized that I had arrived at my desired destination.

I opened the door to Fetzer Hall and ran down the corridor towards my boss's office. I had always prided myself on being on time, something I had learned from my dad, and did not want this particular meeting with Dr. Carson to be the one where I made the wrong impression. Gliding up the final stairwell and cutting crisply around the corner, I had arrived promptly on time for the meeting. With the door slightly ajar, I proceeded to the entry where I heard Dr. Carson at his desk clicking methodically at his keyboard. I knocked two times lightly to signify my arrival as the door edge peeked open just enough to see the inside of his light blue cinder block office.

"Coyte, how's it going?" inquired Dr. Carson as he glided around his desk to greet me. "Good to see you."

"Thanks, you too," I replied as I shook my boss's hand. "I am just curious to hear what we're going to be chatting about."

I had hoped that this comment would elicit a response that would help me deduct the nature of the conversation, but Dr. Carson kept a poker face and did not tip his hand.

"Would you like to sit?" asked Dr. Carson as he pointed to his small conference table. He briefly ran his right hand through his jet-black hair before adding: "There is something I would like to talk to you about."

"Sure," I responded as I promptly sat myself directly across from my boss. "Excited to hear what you have to say."

With both parties seated, Dr. Carson placed an envelope in the middle of the table and shifted slightly in his seat before starting the conversation. "Coyte, you know how I feel about you. Over the past six years, you have been a valuable part of our Sport Administration program and are extremely well liked in our department. I am not just saying that. I have talked to our entire faculty and across the board they feel like you have made a positive contribution in so many areas. I truly mean that."

"Well, I appreciate that Dr. Carson," I responded enthusiastically. Feeling like this was a part of my congratulations speech, I added, "I have truly enjoyed working here. Everyone has been so kind to me since I arrived on campus."

Dr. Carson flinched a little at this comment and paused for a moment. After a couple of silent seconds, he slid the envelope forward on the table.

"This letter in front of you is your tenure decision. As you know, we voted unanimously 14-0 at the departmental level to grant you promotion. This then went up a level where you were fully supported by the college, including our Senior Associate Dean, Dean and committee."

"That's great!" I interjected. "That makes me happy to hear that!"

"Yeah, and you deserve that," implored Dr. Carson. He paused for a second before looking straight into my eyes. "Listen, this is not the conversation I wanted to have with you Coyte.

In an instant, I felt the positivity throughout my body start to drain. At the same time, my heart began to beat rapidly at a hummingbird's pace on the inside of my chest. I waited fearfully to hear my verdict as Dr. Carson paused for a few seconds to gather his thoughts.

"After approval within our college, your application went to the highest level where a university committee took all the input into consideration. Unfortunately, they did not agree with our assessment and voted 7-1 against your application. I am so sorry that I have to be the one to give you this news, but you have been denied tenure."

My face immediately went flush as I failed to come up with a coherent response to the life altering news that had been thrust upon me. I felt as if someone had just sucker punched me in the gut leaving me without the ability to draw a breath. Feeling a little light headed, my mind started to rush about all the ways this decision would impact my family's life.

How will Brandy feel about this?

Will this hurt my ability to get another job?

How will this impact the kids?

There were so many questions running through my mind that I was just not prepared to answer. I was officially in uncharted territory and didn't know my next step.

NAVIGATING UNCHARTED TERRITORY

Nobody ever teaches you in school how to react when you get fired from a job that you truly care about. Come to think of it, that isn't something you learn about at any point in your life. Yet here I was in the middle of this exact situation trying to figure out how to respond in a way that would bring some order to my life. The problem was that my negative emotions were running rampant no matter how hard I tried to control them.

In the days following the decision, I was confused, and admittedly a little shocked, because I had a hard time coming to grip with the fact that the situation was happening to me. I had certainly heard "horror stories" about tenure decisions gone awry, but had never imagined being cast as the victim in this type of script.

This confused stage only lasted a few days. Rather than sit in it, I did what any normal person would do. I started to seek out reasons why this was happening to me. In full disclosure, I was also holding out hope that the decision makers would "see the light" and all of a sudden realize they had made a mistake. I ended up disappointed on both fronts because I did not find the outcomes I was seeking. Instead, the decision remained in place and nobody could give me a strong reason why I had lost my job at the university. The best I got was from a high-level administrator who explained to me that "it was like I was a really good baseball player, but was playing cricket and had no idea that I was playing cricket." This feedback led me to being frustrated and then eventually angry. I couldn't understand why nobody could give me a meaningful reason why my entire life had just been turned upside down after pouring my heart into my job the last six years.

You know the interesting thing? Anger was not even close to being the worst emotion that I experienced after my decision. It was a pit stop on the way to a state that was completely foreign to me. It wasn't until I was watching Brene Brown's TED Talk about a month later that I realized that what I was experiencing was shame. I felt embarrassed going to work each day because I had been fired and everyone around me knew it. My colleagues and students were all supportive and kind, but I still felt disconnected from the group in a way that made me feel like I was not enough. That was definitely the hardest emotion because it caused me to question myself and my abilities. I am not sure I realized it at the time, but I was lost. Then I stumbled upon a lesson that woke me up and put me on an entirely different path.

THE HABIT THAT FLIPPED
MY LIFE RIGHT SIDE UP

I didn't tell you this story to make you feel bad for me. The reality is that many of you have faced similar or more difficult situations in your own life. Adversity can be really daunting because it often leads to negative emotions that you don't necessarily know how to handle. It isn't something that is commonly taught in our society. In the month following my tenure decision, I made some modest attempts to point my brain to positive, but I quickly became discouraged and worn down because I kept getting drawn back into negative patterns.

I now realize that this was because I had the wrong approach initially. It wasn't reasonable to expect a complete turnaround in my situation by intentionally redirecting my negative thoughts one-at-a-time. I have since learned from coaching thousands of people that this just isn't feasible. There is too much going on in our lives for this meticulous redirect approach to work. Flipping the script on one negative thought at a time is a monumental task that will lead most people back to disappointment. Most often, you end up worn down and exhausted because it takes too much ENERGY capacity. This was certainly the case for me. I continued to struggle until I stumbled on a new approach that was far more efficient.

I still remember the exact day I made the critical decision to implement a single habit that got my life back on track. It was a full month after my tenure news and I was sitting in my home office on a warm Spring afternoon looking out over the tall pine trees. I was simultaneously reflecting on my current situation when a profound insight hit me.

I am caught up in a loop of negative thoughts, beliefs and emotions that will never serve me. If I don't create change, I will continue to run into disappointment.

I decided that day alone in my office that it was time to stop feeling sorry for myself. It was on me to step up and give my brain a better option. I was committed to finding a more positive approach so I could get much better results in the future.

Never in a million years could I have ever imagined the profound impact that this one habit would end up having on my life. Here's the honest truth.

One single habit put me back on the path to positive.

One single habit started a journey that taught me the power of choosing my response to any situation I faced in life.

One single habit was the catalyst for the creation of a unique system of world-class habits that helped me flip the script on my biggest barriers.

In hindsight, all I really did to create profound change in my life was get up and pursue the habits outlined in this book. One-by-one, over the next two years, I started to stack these engrained behaviors and they allowed me to flip the script on my biggest barriers. It was honestly never my intention to make this happen at the start of my journey. I just wanted to feel more in control of my life and this was the step-by-step process that emerged to make it happen. I now realize that these powerful habits were officially the start of my "yellow ball" philosophy: *focal points I followed each morning to flip the script on my biggest barriers.* It just now dawned on me that this concept is going to require a little more explanation if we are going to travel somewhere special in this book together.

"CAN YOU GO GET
THE YELLOW BALL?"

Once we made the decision to walk away from academia to pursue my dream of becoming an author, coach and speaker, there was far more flexibility in where we chose to live. For nine years, we had picked our home solely based on university locations. Now we had the opportunity to pull up a United States map and pick our desired living location. After a short 10 month stint in Indiana, we decided to make the trek 2500 miles across the country to the Pacific Northwest. We would be living in Anacortes, Washington, in the gorgeous San Juan Islands, where I had grown up as a child.

It didn't take us long to realize that the move to Washington was an absolute blessing for our family. On more than one occasion, Brandy has told me, "It just feels like we were supposed to be here. It seems like it was meant to be." I have to admit that I completely agree because it has led us to unexpected experiences and lessons that have guided this journey. It has almost seemed like divine intervention at times. One of these arrived on a mild Spring evening two years after my tenure decision while attending swim lessons with our son Carter.

As I walked out of the locker room, I scanned the pool area. *It looks exactly like it did 30-years ago when I was taking my first swim lesson.* Glancing over at Carter, who we call "Cube," I noticed that his arms were pinned to his sides and his body was stiff as a board. There was no question in my mind that he was more than a little nervous so I put my hand on his shoulder and shot him a smile.

Right about this time, Trevor, one of the most enthusiastic high school students I had ever met, strolled up and introduced himself. "What's u-p-p-p Carter?!?!" he bellowed passionately while raising his hand up promptly for a big high five. "You ready to swim-m-m-m buddy?!?!" Noticing that Carter had immediately relaxed after this introduction, I became intrigued by this 18-year old's eccentric approach.

After guiding the students to the edge of the pool, Trevor asked each of them to get into the water onto a platform. He proceeded to do an interactive warm-up session that allowed the group of six-year olds to get more comfortable with the water. It was about 10-minutes in when I noticed that Trevor was pointing to another platform about eight feet from the first one. I paid close attention and heard him tell the students that he wanted them to try to swim to the other platform all by themselves. He was going to be there to help them if needed, but they would be all on their own initially in this pursuit.

Carter and the rest of the gang instantly slid back and gripped the edge of the pool for safety. I could tell from their reaction that fear had clearly entered the equation. I knew exactly how they felt because I had felt the same way 30 years earlier in my first swim lesson. I was a wild kid that my parents said had "no fear," but this wasn't entirely true. I remember distinctly being scared at my swimming lessons. I guess there is something about not coming back up in water deeper than your head that catches your brain's attention and signals a fear and flight response.

I know I am supposed to be the motivational guy, but in this moment, I saw no way that Trevor could pull this off with this group of terrified six-year olds. *ZERO percent chance he gets them to willingly jump into that water. This dude is officially out of his mind.* Those were the honest first thoughts that popped into my mind. Sensing their hesitation, Trevor walked over to the edge of the pool where he grabbed a slightly oversized, yellow rubber ball. After shaking it back and forth in front of their faces, he threw it up and down methodically as each of the kid's heads bobbed up and down as they tracked it. Then he paused for a moment with a smirk on his face as he asked them, "Do you think you can catch it?"

I think you can guess how a young kid would respond to this question. Every single one of them cheerfully replied, "Yea-a-a-a-h!" Without hesitation, he started to throw the ball to each of them one-by-one as they caught it and returned it to him. Once he had established that they could clearly catch the ball and built up their confidence, Trevor turned to the other platform and threw the ball directly in its vicinity. "Do you think you can go get the ball?" he asked them with the same smirk on his face. This question piqued my interest as I was curious to hear their response.

With literally no hesitation in their voice, every single kid gave him a similar enthusiastic "Yea-a-a-ah!" response.

Wait, what?!?! No, that can't be right! No way those kids will jump into that water just because he waved a yellow ball in front of them!

I watched with fascination as my son Carter proceeded to dive into the water and swim, or I guess you could say it was more like flailing, to chase down the yellow ball. Yet this flailing led him to the other side where Trevor helped him up on the platform to retrieve this magical yellow ball. Carter immediately turned to me with a big old smile on his face and gave me a thumbs up.

I shook my head in disbelief reflecting on what I had just witnessed. I realized that what he had accomplished was nothing short of remarkable. This animated, quirky 18-year old high school student had made fear disappear instantly in a group of six-year olds. Not only that, he had done it without ever telling them there was nothing to worry about. No conversations whatsoever. Trevor had simply given them something exciting to focus on that piqued their brain's interest and redirected it away from what they were initially scared of. Then he used this focal point to guide the kids towards an end outcome that they didn't think was possible. Not a single kid had even realized what had happened. I'm not convinced any parent even grasped the magnitude of what Trevor had pulled off.

As I left the pool that day, I reminisced on the significance of what I had just witnessed. It was a flippin Houdini act! With a single yellow ball, he had helped every one of those kids break through a prominent mental barrier with ease. This was the same emotional state that was robbing most adults of their ability to achieve their desired goals and dream lives. My mind immediately started to become consumed with a single thought:

Is it possible to do the exact same thing with grown adults? Can you make fear disappear with a yellow ball?

I know what you might be thinking. *Yeah, Coyte. If you took me to a pool, I could flippin jump in and chase down a yellow ball too. Come on dude. I didn't pick up your book to be badgered!* Listen, I'm with you 100 percent. I believe you are totally capable of making that happen, but we both know that isn't what is at stake here. What I am talking about is something so much more profound. It is the ability to make self-doubt, fear and other prominent barriers that rob us of our highest potential disappear with the right focal points. This is when another profound question popped in my mind:

If I came up with the right yellow balls designed to flip the script on prominent barriers, could I pull this off and help people pull out their highest potential?

There is something incredible that happens in life when you get in the habit of asking yourself the right questions. The moment I posed this query to my brain with emotional curiosity, I immediately knew the answer to my own question. There was no hesitation in my response. It was an unequivocal, non-debatable "yes" in my mind. Why? I had just experienced this exact situation in my own life. Almost two years earlier, I had faced a major challenge in my professional career that turned my family's life upside down. It was in the middle of this adversity that I had found my own yellow balls. I had simply chased them every single day and this allowed me to flip my mindset and life back right side up.

THE FLIPPIN POINT

So, what's the flippin point here? The point is that in the middle of pain I learned a powerful process that allowed me to flip the script on my biggest barriers in life. By simply following 10 yellow ball habits, I trained my brain to go from dwelling on disappointment to pursuing my purpose, passion and potential all out in a two-year period. I have since used this same process to continue to radically elevate my productivity and performance in the key areas of my life. It has been so impactful that I have now coached these strategies to thousands of people all across the United States. I have seen similar transformations in clients who have chased the yellow balls consistently in their own lives. *That's the flippin point.*

During my journey, I have come to realize that the barriers I faced in my journey are not at all uncommon in our society. Instead, I have learned that most people are being robbed of the ability to live to their highest potential by the same exact obstacles. Distractions, fear, fitting in, instant gratification, perfection and self-doubt pretty much impact every single person on the planet at some point in their lives. But they don't have to if you implement habits that point your brain to productive on a consistent daily basis. It is completely within your power to give your mind a better option that pulls out your highest potential. *That's the flippin point.*

If there is one thing I have learned on my journey, it is that single habits have the power to radically transform your mindset and life. That is, if you have the discipline and toughness to follow through on them every single day regardless of whether you feel like it or not. If you are looking for better options in your life, it is my hope that you will find them within the pages of this book. All it takes is one habit to create a subtle shift that starts to lead your life to a place that you never previously imagined possible. For now, all you have to do to make this happen is read on and commit to chasing the yellow balls at the end of each chapter. If all goes well, you will learn what it means to truly flip the script in your life as you pull out your highest potential and create a life you absolutely love. *That's the flippin point.*

66-DAYS...BURDEN OR BARGAIN?

Throughout this book, I am going to challenge you to embrace profound habits with the power to transform your mindset and life. These will be habits custom designed to help you flip the script on your biggest barriers so you can pull out your highest potential. I want to point out that every single one of these habits came from a combination of research, reflection and extensive repetition. Being completely transparent up front, these are not habits that are easy to come by. With each one, you are going to have to show up and follow through on your intentions even when you don't feel like it. I always make this clear when doing keynote talks on these powerful habits.

There comes a point in the talk when I need to outline what it will take to establish a habit so that a new neural pathway forms in their brain. This leads to the behavior becoming second nature and requires much less ENERGY to follow through on their intentions. Rather than draining capacity, this is the point where these transformational habits actually drive your clarity, focus, motivation, passion and vitality on a daily basis. Do you know how long this takes? Science has shown that this occurs anywhere between 21 and 66 days. I always err on the safe side by estimating high. In my experiences, this is generally the time when most people feel they have their behavior fully locked in.

Every time I mention the amount of time it takes to establish a habit, I can just see the disappointment well up in audience members' eyes. In an instant gratification driven society, this seems like an eternity for some people. One time I actually had someone raise her hand before blurting out, "66-days… that's a lon-n-n-n-g time. It seems like a bit much." I had to pause for a moment to determine how to respond to this person. I wasn't ready to respond in a productive manner that day, but I am now. It all has to do with perspective and you need to decide how you will see this decision.

When I finally had time to reflect, here was my thought process.

It takes 66-days to establish a profound habit designed to help you become more positive.

In a little over a two-month period, you can lock in an automated behavior that will set the tone for better results and allow you to close the gap on your desired outcomes.

In the process, this habit can also help you radically elevate your emotions, intentional action and quality of life.

This is the same habit that will drive clarity, ENERGY, motivation, passion and results in the key areas of your life.

Wait, it only takes 66-days?!?! You can literally change the entire trajectory of your life by showing up and fighting for it in 1/6th of a calendar year.

Now that's a flippin bargain!

The issue with some of the audience members I mentioned is that they were looking at these habits the wrong way. They had framed them in a way that made them seem like a burden. With this perspective, they would always avoid any productive behavior with the potential to radically transform their lives. All I had done was change the narrative so that these habits seemed like an incredible opportunity. I learned to hack my brain so it moved willingly towards new behaviors that allowed me to flip the script on my biggest barriers. And it only took me 66-days to start making it happen!

You need to decide right now how you will see these yellow ball habits when they are presented to you.

Are they a burden or bargain?

When the 66-day time period pops up in a chapter, I hope you will make a conscious decision to choose a productive perspective. Let's be straight, though. It's a flippin bargain! I hope you will take these deals and make a decision to run with them. If you do this often enough, I truly believe it will lead you to a place where you absolutely love the view in your life.

CHAPTER 1

FL!P
ING
NEGATIVE NOISE

MASTER AN NTT MORNING GROWTH ROUTINE

"When you spend the early hours energizing yourself, you get pulled through the rest of your day with little additional effort. Structuring the early hours of each day is the simplest way to extraordinary results."
—Gary Keller

I was browsing the Internet one day when I came upon a statistic that absolutely BLEW MY MIND. Do you want to hear it? Try this one on for size: the average person has up to 80% of their thoughts that are negative in a single day. This sounded like a pretty big statistic, but I wanted to grasp the implications of this on our lives so I did a little number crunching to give it some context. This seemingly unreasonable statistic meant that a large chunk of our population was walking around with up to 40,000 negative thoughts bouncing around in their brains each day. This was the equivalent of having 12.8 hours of counterproductive thoughts in a 16-hour awake period and 4,672 hours in a year. That's when it hit me that most people are wasting a majority of their waking moments on thoughts that are creating a disappointing drag on their lives.

I still remember the first thought that came to mind when reading these statistics. *WHA-A-A-A-A-A-A-T?!?! Nah-h-h-h, that can't possibly be accurate!*

That's outrageous! As outlandish as it sounded, I quickly came to the realization that it was totally true once I did some research and paid attention to people's behaviors.

The second thought that came to mind was, *Yeah, but that's NOT me! I'm a pretty positive person!* I honestly just assumed that this amount of negative was reserved for "other" people. I guess I just figured that I wouldn't be a part of this statistic since I had always worked to keep a more productive demeanor.

I decided that I would track my thoughts for an entire day just to confirm my positive nature. It made sense for me to flip the script on any negative thoughts even if I only had a select few occupying my brain on a consistent daily basis. I anticipated that this would give me the opportunity to increase my efficiency a smidge and this certainly couldn't hurt. Once I had done this, I could show people with more prominent negative thoughts how to make similar shifts. I determined that I would start this tracking process immediately the next morning.

As I stumbled out of bed and headed downstairs, I realized that my mind was already bouncing around like a ping pong ball contemplating all the things I needed to get done in my day. I noticed that this led me to a feeling of unease in my stomach as I transitioned into my morning routine. Just as I got settled in with my book on the couch, Carter, my three-year old son at the time, came roaring downstairs and immediately demanded breakfast. When I told him to wait a second, he ERRUPTED like an angry volcano when responding, "NO-O-O-O-O-O, my tummy hurts daddy! NOW-W-W-W-W-W!!!"

Once he calmed down a few minutes later, I headed to the kitchen to get him some food. But not until I had clearly shown him my frustration and used some choice words under my breath. *I swear, this kid is a savage! Little dude needs to learn some flippin manners,* I thought as I marched out of the living room to retrieve some peanut butter, toast and fresh water.

As I arrived in the kitchen, I noticed a tall glass that had a small amount of purple-ish smoothie festering in it from the previous day. *Are you kidding me...again Brandy?!?! How many times are you going to do this?!?! So-o-o-o-o-o nasty... and freakin selfish!!!*

Once I finished my breakfast, I rushed out of my house and hopped into my Toyota Tacoma to race to campus. Glancing at my clock, I realized that I would have just enough time to stop by my office to print out some papers before rushing upstairs to teach my class. It seemed like it was all going to work out.

Just then, I glanced up at the approaching traffic light that switched unexpectedly to orange. *A-h-h-h-h man-n-n-n-n*, I thought. *Why does this ALWAYS happen to me when I am short on time? Damn light!!!*

Just as I regained my optimal traveling speed and composure, a red Ford Taurus cut right in front of me without warning, causing me to pump my breaks. I could immediately feel my fight response boiling up in my body.

Come on dude!!! What is wrong with you?!?! Have some freakin manners!!!

My nostrils flared and my heart pounded rapidly inside of my chest. I tried to shake it off, but I couldn't seem to let go of this small, meaningless traffic incident. I felt like I had been cheated out of something.

My negative emotions carried over as I rushed across the turf field to my office. After just barely having enough time to print my papers, I ran upstairs towards my classroom. Marching down the final corridor, I could feel a nervousness building up in the pit of my stomach.

I really don't feel like teaching today. I wish I could just go back to my office and come back Wednesday feeling fresh.

This was the first time I consciously noticed the dread response I had for teaching. The strange thing is that I had always prided myself on loving adding value to students. Yet here I was focused on all the reasons I didn't want to go in and work with an incredible group of gifted young human beings.

I only needed until noon to realize that I had a serious problem on my hands.

In a little less than a six-hour period, I had shattered my previous belief that I was a positive person who was immune from the staggering statistics on the seemingly never-ending negative thoughts. This simple activity had brought to my attention a myriad of counterproductive patterns that were creating a serious drag on my results and life. On impulse, I was unfairly judging my hungry three-year old. I was cursing my wife about a leftover smoothie when she does 99% of all the household tasks and is pretty much a saint. I was telling myself I was the "add value" guy, and here I was, dreading the gift I had to teach my class.

It dawned on me that I was wasting a sizable chunk of time and ENERGY on habits that could have been allocated to closing the gap on my desired outcomes in life. I knew it was time to come up with a better approach to get control over my mindset. I just wasn't quite sure yet exactly what that would be. A full month had near passed since my tenure decision and it was time to step up and give my brain a better option.

THE PAIN OF THE NEVER-ENDING NEGATIVE NOISE

I was sitting in my office a few days after my eye-opening tracking activity reflecting on my current situation. I knew I was caught up in a loop of negative thoughts and emotions that were creating unnecessary tension in my life. I decided that it was time for a change. I had been listening to a podcast episode with Tony Robbins when he mentioned that pain was one of the strongest leverage points to drive human behavior. *Maybe that is the key to interrupting my current negative patterns?* I thought to myself. I decided right that moment that it would serve me to get crystal clear on the consequences of continuing with my current negative thought patterns. It was time to stack the deck so change became a must.

It didn't take me long doing research to come up with some pain points that caught my attention. Not surprisingly, negative thoughts have been shown to lead to negative emotions in human beings. So, when you focus 80 percent of your time dwelling on counterproductive thoughts, it is pretty much guaranteed that you will end up habitually experiencing undesirable emotions like anger, disappointment, frustration, overwhelm and sadness. If you do this often enough, you can actually train your brain and the cells in your body to get addicted to these emotional states and they become your norm. *That doesn't sound good to me at all, I thought. I am not willing to live the rest of my life dwelling on disappointment.*

Looking at some additional studies, I found that negative thoughts and emotions also create a drain on your clarity and focus. Every time you fall into the pattern of emphasizing negative, it takes away valuable time that could have been allocated to your most important things. On top of this, it creates a drain on your ENERGY levels that leaves you feeling completely worn down throughout your days, weeks and months. To cap things off, research has actually shown that negative thinking leads to stress that lowers the effectiveness of your body's immune system. It turns out that the wrong thoughts can actually increase your risk of heart disease and other outcomes that radically lower your quality of life.

All of these really started to make me realize that I needed to fight to create change in my life. But do you know the one pain point that really spoke to me and made change a must? It actually didn't come from any research. It stemmed from the realization that I was wasting my life with these patterns. It finally dawned on me that if I allowed even 50 percent of my thoughts to be negative, I had NO SHOT of ever doing anything remarkable and memorable with my life. That was never going to be all right for me. I had finally found a cost I was not willing to pay. I knew I would never accept settling for the status quo and leaving so much potential on the table.

WHAT IF?
IMAGINE THE POSSIBILITIES...

I always smile on the inside when giving a keynote talk and outline the seemingly never-ending nature of negative thoughts. You can just sense the audience cultivating an intrigue and concern as you lay out the prominence and implications of counterproductive habits on our lives. I don't smile because I enjoy putting them into an alarmed state. That would be a little sadistic. I smile because I know the radical turn we are about to take on our journey. I always joke that if I stopped before this point, I could make a strong argument for being one of the best de-motivational speakers on the market.

Here is what I know. The previous statistics and costs are simply a short pit stop as we fuel up for a wild road trip we are about to take together. I absolutely LOV-V-V-V-E this part because it is the exact moment where overwhelm starts to magically morph into opportunity. This is the pivot point where I see lights go off in people's heads because they start to fully grasp the incredible potential they have in front of them to create radical change in their lives. This is the precise time when we talk about the unlimited capacity they have to break their counterproductive habits and pull out their highest potential.

What if you could flip the script on all of your negative patterns and use every single minute of your days to close the gap on the exact results you desire? Just imagine the possibilities.

Instead of 40,000 negative thoughts dragging you down each day, you could reallocate all of this ENERGY and capacity to empowering habits that would radically elevate your quality of life.

Rather than choosing 12.8 hours of disappointing beliefs that are not serving any meaningful purpose, you could redirect your full attention towards goals and values that would give you uplifting emotions that would make your life vibrant.

And in place of the 4,672 hours given to unproductive thoughts, beliefs and emotions, you could tap into the deep inner desire that you have as a human being to go out and create results and a life you absolutely love.

Pretty neat to consider the possibility!

THE LAW OF FIRSTS

I have a good friend named Ken Hubbard who has been doing leadership training for over 30-years of his life. There are several of his lessons that I love, but one of my all-time favorites that I have learned from him has been "The Law of Firsts." In our interactions, he has consistently emphasized the importance of prioritizing top values in your day-to-day life. I have heard him say several times, "If something truly matters, it will show up in your calendar, focus and resources." I was reflecting on this thought one afternoon when I realized that there was another profound implication to this law. It had to do with the thing you prioritize in one of the most important times in your day.

Whenever I get the chance to visit with audiences while doing keynote talks, I make a point to ask them about their routine in the morning. "What's the very first thing you do when you wake up?" I ask them. I remember the first time I decided to present this question to a live audience. I was feeling pretty clever because I was certain they would give me the response I was looking for. It would go something like this: "Well, I am so glad you asked Coyte. I check my cell phone." Wrong! I had been off base in my initial assessment.

Do you know the first thing people actually do when they wake up? Yep, people tend to instinctively hit the snooze button and roll out of bed to pee.

I have to admit that I should have seen that coming. You can imagine my surprise and smidge of embarrassment when I realized I had been off in my perceived expert assessment. That is, until it came to my attention that a lot of people multi-task during their morning bathroom release. What is it that people commonly do while on the pot? *Ding, ding, ding!* You likely guessed it. They often take their cell phones with them and get all caught up on their social media, emails and favorite site updates. I know, gross, but it is the truth that most people have done it at least once at some point in the last few weeks!

You might be saying to yourself, "Ok, Coyte. Maybe that's true, but what's the big deal? So what if I use my cell phone first thing in the morning?" I honestly believe I would have instinctively said the same thing about five years ago. I was wrong then and I'll tell you why.

Do you remember the "Law of Firsts" we just discussed? Well, it turns out that our brain is very good at focusing on the things that we prioritize in our life. While there are several firsts to consider, one of the most important is what you choose to point your brain to immediately when you wake up. Why? It essentially sets the mental tone for your entire day. When your automated response is social media, prominent news sites or trending television shows, you are essentially training your brain to find and focus on junk because these options are commonly littered with negative messages.

The truth is that I was doing this exact thing in my life. I was waking up each morning and allowing my devices to set the tone for my day. It's no wonder that I was caught in a loop of negative noise.

It was time to give myself a little tough love. Nothing was going to magically change my negative thoughts until I eliminated my harmful morning habits.

But I also sensed that there was more to it than that. I needed to do so much better than just avoiding doing the wrong things. This was a status quo standard that would lead me straight down a path to mediocrity. I needed to aim a lot higher than that to get the life I knew I was meant to be living. It was time to give my brain an empowering morning option that would pull out my highest potential. That's where a magical new routine came into play.

THE MAGIC OF
THE NTT MORNING GROWTH ROUTINE

You have already heard me reference the fact that one habit started this entire process that allowed me to flip the script on the biggest barriers in my life. I didn't clearly identify this habit prior to now because I wanted to create a little drama and incentivize you to read on with intrigue. Well, now is the time to roll it out. *Drum roll please...*

In the middle of my tenure decision when caught in a loop of negativity, the choice I made was to get up early at 5:00am every single morning to read empowering books. I guess you could say that it was a hybrid, "two-habits-in-one" power combo: (1) rise early and (2) read. Then I simply repeated this daily growth behavior until it was second nature.

This ended up being one of the single best decisions I have ever made in my life. Why? Because it started to point my brain to positive consistently and planted the seed for realizing that you can train your brain to focus on pretty much anything. It was also at this critical time that I started to capitalize on "The Law of Firsts." Rather than allowing social media and technology to set the tone in my day, I had the opportunity to dictate the pace by putting powerful thoughts in my brain that were in alignment with my purpose and potential. It didn't take me long after implementing this reading habit to notice that I was definitely focusing more on positive thoughts and outcomes.

There was a second powerful benefit that came out of this morning routine. It was another outcome that I never anticipated and didn't realize its impact until after the fact. As I got up each morning, I had made a decision to invest in myself. This might not seem like much at first glance, but it is such a critical investment. At a time when I was doubting myself, I had started to get up at an "unreasonable" time to invest in ME. Every time I followed through, I was doing more than cultivating my skill sets. I was proving to myself that I was capable of showing up and earning remarkable results in my life. This paid massive dividends for me as I moved further along in my journey.

The third benefit that came from this morning growth routine was a "Sacred Space" concept that now drives every top value area in my life. Rather than mail it in, this became a "No Technology Time" (NTT) where I put my phone away and focused solely on reading, self-improvement and enhancing my life. At a time when most of the world was quiet, I was up investing in a process that became sacred to me. It was in this time frame that I fought for focus and regained my ability to lock in on the things that mattered to me most. This also paved the road for incredible gains in the remaining flips outlined in this book.

Honestly, if you could have told me 10 years ago that waking up at 5:00am was a magical time to transform your life, I would have thought you were insane. Yet once you do it for an extended period of time, something truly remarkable starts to happen in your life. In the silent moments while the rest of the world is soundly snoozing, you start to gradually train your brain to believe that more is "possible" in your life. When everything is quiet in your household, this is the exact time when you give yourself the opportunity to lock in on your most important things and find the next level. It is during these moments that your morning routine will start to morph mundane into magical in your life.

WHY GROWTH IS SO GREAT

It only took me about a week to realize that my morning routine was radically changing my perspective towards my tenure situation. The previous unsuccessful attempts to redirect away from negative to positive were now naturally occurring far more frequently in my days. This made me realize that I had far more control over my thoughts and emotions than I previously imagined. I just needed to continue to invest in my morning growth routine so I could hone this skill set. Once I realized what was at stake, there was no returning. The benefits of growth were far too great to ignore. I made daily personal growth an absolute must moving forward. Outside of marrying my wife and deciding to have our kids, I am not sure I have made a more crucial commitment in my life.

In hindsight, I now realize that I was flat out worn down at the start of this process. I have to admit that there was a part of me that was a little optimistic that my morning routine would help increase my ENERGY levels. I completely underestimated the potential here. I had no idea that re-gaining control of my mind would lead to such a radical shift in my ENERGY levels throughout my days. As I honed my capacity to focus on productive in my environment, I became increasingly excited about the potential to create change in my life. This is when I connected another magical component related to cultivating a growth mindset. *The right activities, once they become habit, turn into powerful chargers that help you radically improve focus and vitality in your life.*

It only took me a month to get hooked on my morning growth routine. But there was one final shift that sealed the deal on growth becoming a core identify for me. With each morning rep that I logged, there was a profound paradigm shift that was taking place in my brain. You see, I loved the benefits I was reaping from my investments so much that growth naturally became an absolute top value in my life. Rather than being overly consumed by external accomplishments and what they meant for me, I was starting to see things from a growth mindset. This meant that I could let my guard down and just start pursuing my dreams with a passion to get better.

This might not seem like a transformational shift, but it was absolutely a game changer for me. Rather than dwell on all the things outside of my control, I now had a focal point that I could pursue regardless of my circumstances and environment. No matter what was going on in my life, I could always show up and give my absolute best effort to grow each day. Regardless of the outcome, it was always possible to find new ways to improve and close the gap on my highest potential. I started to realize that it was possible for me to value growth in a way that would begin to make fear disappear and completely free me up to pursue my dream life. It wasn't my initial intention, but within a few short months, I had stumbled on one of the most powerful programming shifts to live a remarkable life.

WHAT'S FLIPPIN AT STAKE?

I honestly had no idea exactly what was at stake when I started this journey. I just knew I wanted to give my brain a better option than anger, frustration and shame. It's possible that you are in a similar position at this exact moment. Maybe you have been struggling in your life and you are ready for so much better. Or it is possible that you are doing pretty well and you are passionate about finding an entirely different level. Regardless, one of the keys to making this happen is maximizing the use of your time, ENERGY and brain capacity. It is impossible to do this if you are overwhelmed with negative noise on a consistent daily basis.

I now understand exactly what is at stake when you embark on this journey. In front of you is a simple decision with the potential to change your life forever.

Will you show up for yourself every single day?

That is the question you must answer as you start this journey.

There will be times when you don't feel like it so you need to make this decision right now.

Are you willing to fight to make investing in yourself an absolute top priority?

There is something magical that happens when you decide to show up and invest in yourself every single day. If your answer is "yes" to these questions, then you are ready to start a journey with the potential to radically transform your mindset and life.

What's really at stake here? Whether or not you are going to commit to pulling out your highest potential. Regardless of your situation, the choice to invest in yourself is one that will ultimately determine what you achieve and experience in life. It can seem like a benign decision in the moment, but don't be fooled because there is flippin a lot at stake right now with this choice.

Settling or striving for potential.

Ordinary or extraordinary.

Mundane or magical.

Let life keep controlling you or you take control of your life.

With each day that you pass on pursuing your highest potential, you are giving up gifts that lie deep inside of you waiting to get out. It is time to make a decision to flip the script on negative noise so you can cultivate a growth mindset that allows you to CRUSH IT in your life moving forward.

FLIPPIN NEGATIVE THOUGHTS

Are you flippin sick of allowing negative noise to dictate the pace in your life? I sure hope so because there are literally no tangible benefits to holding onto negative patterns that are significantly diminishing your clarity, focus, ENERGY, productivity and potential on a consistent daily basis. When I finally realized just how many negative thoughts were mindlessly filtering through my brain each day, I was absolutely stunned. Then I proceeded to temporarily be a little discouraged because I realized that I had wasted so much time on worthless thoughts and emotions. However, I refused to allow myself to get permanently stuck in this negative pattern. This is when I fought to give my brain a better option with my NTT Morning Growth Routine.

It was in the middle of this new habit that I realized the opportunity I had in front of me. The opportunity to take back significant chunks of time and ENERGY to allocate to my desired outcomes in life. The opportunity to intentionally point my brain to productive so I could create empowering emotions that would make my life remarkable and memorable. The opportunity to start finding ways to use every single minute to flip the script on my biggest barriers so I could pull out my highest potential. I got good at flooding my brain with opportunity so it was excited for the chance to create meaningful transformation moving forward.

I hope you can see the incredible opportunity that lies in front of you. There is no logical reason to spend even one more single minute on negative. Every single time you flip the script on a negative thought pattern, you cast a vote for living to your highest potential. On top of this, you buy back time and ENERGY to allocate to the values and outcomes that matter to you most. All you have to do right now to start making this happen is chase this first yellow ball. Get up every single morning and make you a priority so you can flip the script on negative and make positive and productive your norm.

YELLOW BALL #1:

THE "NTT MORNING GROWTH ROUTINE" HABIT

If there is one thing I have learned from working with thousands of people on this process, it is that simplicity is the key to transformation. The moment things get fancy and complicated, people tend to draw back and fall into old, counterproductive habits. This is why we are going to keep things simple in this book. We don't need a 10-point plan right now to flip the script on negative noise in your life. This would just overwhelm you and put you in an emotional state where you questioned the process and your ability to create change. What we need is one single yellow ball for you to chase. The type that anyone can go out and pursue if they are motivated to do so…but minus the whole pool thing and without an actual yellow ball.

Are you ready for it? Here you go.

Determine an exact time that you will get up every single morning to read empowering books for 15-30 minutes for the next 66-days. As you determine this time, flood your brain with all the reasons why you are excited to flip the script on negative in your life. Do this until you can feel yourself fired up about the process you are implementing. Each night before you go to sleep, remind yourself why you are getting up so you prime yourself to rise with the right mindset towards your new habit. It is important that you make this new process pleasurable so your brain is incentivized to pursue it.

Then rise each morning and head to your special spot in your house to perform your reading ritual. Be excited because you now have an opportunity to rewire how your brain perceives and approaches the world. Remind yourself that when emotion enters the equation, it will take this activity to a transformational level and speed up your habit formation process. You will learn more about this throughout the book.

For now, that's it. Rise early and read this book. Make it an absolute must to chase this yellow ball all out so you cultivate a growth mindset that drives powerful change in your life moving forward.

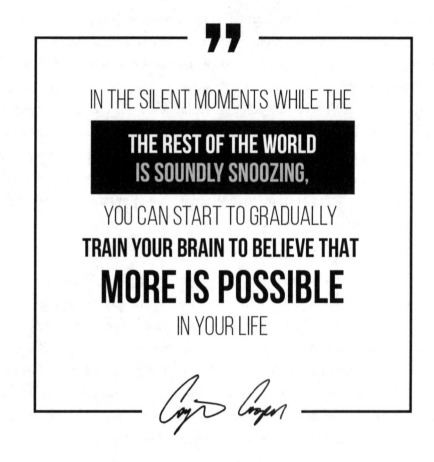

IN THE SILENT MOMENTS WHILE THE

**THE REST OF THE WORLD
IS SOUNDLY SNOOZING,**

YOU CAN START TO GRADUALLY

TRAIN YOUR BRAIN TO BELIEVE THAT

MORE IS POSSIBLE

IN YOUR LIFE

SCARCITY

BUILD YOUR BASELINE BLESSINGS

"Be thankful for what you have; you'll end up having more. If you concentrate on what you don't have, you will never, ever have enough."

—Oprah Winfrey

I shouldn't be where I am at right now. Not after everything I have poured into my career the last nine years. At the age of 34, I was supposed to be advancing in rank to become a tenured, Associate Professor at University of North Carolina. This was meant to be the moment where I went home to celebrate with Brandy because we had achieved a big goal. I had always imagined this being a time when all the hard work we had invested would pay off and I would be set in my career. After all, I had spent four years grinding to earn my Ph.D. and another eight pouring into becoming a tenured professor at one of the top academic institutions in the United States. I felt like I had done everything they had asked me to do throughout the process. I had consistently put in extra work and taken on additional duties to try to improve the program. Now what did I have to show for it? Absolutely nothing.

Nobody likes to admit it, but there is a tendency to dwell on disappointment when we fall short of expectations. I know this was certainly true for me following my tenure decision. Even as my morning growth routine locked into place, I found myself in a negative loop where I was focused on scarcity. Naturally, this was creating an unnecessary drag on my life. Fortunately, my reading ritual led me to a profound insight that unveiled the next step in my journey. It was an unexpected perspective shift that came a few weeks after my tenure decision when I had forgotten to order a new set of books from Amazon.

I had just finished Andy Andrew's *The Travelers Gift* and realized that I didn't have a new book to read. I decided to head to my bookshelf to find something to re-read until my stock was replenished. As I scrolled my shelves, I kept being drawn back to a title that piqued my attention: *Man's Search for Meaning* by Viktor Frankl. It was a book that had initially been recommended to me by 21x NCAA Champion soccer coach Anson Dorrance. He had told me that it was so powerful that he had all of his girls read it as a group to teach them lessons on perspective. For some reason, I couldn't shake the pull to this title, so I picked it up and headed to my couch to start reading.

It didn't take me long to be reminded of the power of the words within this compact book. While I had already read it once before, this time was different because of my situation. It was a message that I desperately needed to hear. Isn't it interesting how life sometimes gives you the exact message you need to hear, at the exact moment you need to hear it, and from the exact source you need to hear it from? If any one of these three elements would have been off, it might have been a lesson that blew right by me like a warm summer breeze. Fortunately it arrived at just the right time. I guess you could say that it was meant to be. Or maybe my subconscious brain is more capable than I give it credit for. The point is that I received the exact lesson I needed to get my mind back on track.

As I settled in for my new growth routine, Dr. Frankl outlined the inhumane conditions he faced after being placed in a concentration camp along with his entire family in 1942. It was hard for me to fathom people being treated so horrifically, let alone being tortured and murdered because of their background.

One-by-one, most of Frankl's family members were killed in these camps. I don't know about you, but I am quite certain I would have lost my marbles if this happened to me. I think I would have had so much pent up rage inside me that I would have gone after the people that took my family members. Yet in the middle of this chaos, he didn't do this at all. Instead, he made a remarkable decision that completely shaped the magnificence of his life.

Rather than dwell on his circumstances, he chose to give his brain a productive outcome by focusing on helping newcomers cope with the shock of transitioning into these grotesque camps. He then went out of his way to organize suicide prevention groups to try and improve the survival rates of concentration camp members. It was in the midst of this devastation that he established his "power of choice" philosophy that allowed him to survive camp and go on to impact millions of lives across the world. It was his intentional response amid this turmoil that allowed him to spread this profound message: "Everything can be taken from a human being but one thing: the last of the human freedoms – to choose one's attitude in any given set of circumstances, to choose one's own way."

I couldn't help but be blown away by Dr. Frankl's response. Here is a guy that had his entire family unjustly robbed from him and he somehow managed to choose a productive response that radically improved his situation and quality of life. It seemed completely unreasonable to me. Yet in the middle of it all, there was a profound weight in his decision that I was curiously drawn towards. Upon reading this "power of choice" journey for a second time, I knew that I only had one reasonable response available to me in my current situation. *If Viktor Frankl could find the gift in the middle of one of life's most devastating situations, I could certainly choose a productive response to my tenure decision.* I had no idea that this single distinction would be the start of an incredible process that allowed me to flip the script on scarcity and some of the biggest barriers in my life.

THE POWER OF PERSPECTIVE

There is no question that Viktor Frankl's "power of choice" philosophy had a powerful impact on my life. It became the foundational driver for this entire flip the script process. If you have a choice on how to respond to your environment, which you do, then why not choose something productive that increases your quality of life? His story taught me that I could always pick a productive response to any situation that life sent my way. This definitely meant changing how I perceived and responded to my tenure decision. I think you will see this play out throughout this entire book.

But there was another powerful lesson that emerged from reading *Man's Search for Meaning*. As I mulled over his circumstances and his "unreasonable" response to them, there was a powerful thought that emerged in my mind that radically changed my entire emotional state. Do you want to hear what it was? Of course you do! That is why you are reading this book after all.

I'm kind of being a baby right now.

Here I am dwelling on losing my job when there are people facing challenges right now in the world that I can't even comprehend dealing with.

It was the first time that I actually realized that perspective could single handedly power my attitude and behaviors.

I am not trying to diminish the severity of losing a job. It's challenging. No question about that. But I also realized that the level of difficulty depended on how I chose to see it. Yes, I had lost a job that I loved, but I still had an incredible wife and two kids downstairs who loved me unconditionally.

Perspective.

It's totally true that I no longer had the financial security that came with a normal career, but I had all the skill sets necessary to go out and pursue my dream life.

Perspective.

And yeah, I wasn't going to have the prestige of being affiliated with a top university, but I didn't need that to pursue my purpose in life.

Perspective.

This taught me that I could always choose my perspective point with some intentional effort. It also made me realize that there were all kinds of reasons around me to feel blessed. I knew at this exact moment that I had a powerful choice to make. I could continue to focus on scarcity and all the things I no longer had in my life or I could intentionally shift my attention to abundance and all the blessings in my life. One decision would guarantee disappointment and the other would give me a shot to pull out my passion and highest potential. It seemed like a pretty clear decision to me at the time.

I didn't realize it at this moment, but this was the official start of one of the most powerful yellow ball habits in the entire flip the script process. It was this profound perspective shift that led me to my baseline blessings. These were the gifts that were currently present in my life that I could always choose to focus on. By giving them my attention, I could get myself into a state of gratitude and abundance that would drive much better emotions and results in my life. Rather than leave this to chance, I decided to make it a habit to revisit them every single day. I wanted to make sure I programmed them properly into my subconscious brain so it would find them no matter what life sent my way.

BUILD YOUR BASELINE BLESSINGS

Why are these baseline blessings so important? Well, in the words of Oprah Winfrey, "If you concentrate on what you don't have, you will never, ever have enough." I believe this to be true to my core. Think about it. When you get in the habit of consistently focusing on scarcity, you are essentially training your subconscious brain to expect this exact thing in your life. It eventually becomes a self-fulfilling prophecy. The more I was focused on what I didn't have following my tenure decision, the more likely I was to attract more disappointment in the future.

How did I give my brain a better option? Baseline blessings. I started to show up in my morning growth routine and reminded my brain of three things I was incredibly blessed to have in my life. It didn't take me long at all to start feeling better. I began to tap into higher level emotions such as gratitude and joy as I emotionally connected to the gifts in my life. As I flooded my brain with blessings, I could tell that my mind was naturally getting better at seeking out the good on its own in the environment around me. I now realize that this simple activity was also training my brain to expect that great things would happen in the future.

Do you know the most powerful shift that came from this baseline blessings habit? It made me realize that I already had more than enough in my life. I didn't need anything else outside of my control to be happy. If I wanted to be fulfilled, I simply needed to stop and acknowledge the fact that I was extremely blessed to already have incredible gifts in my life. The fascinating thing is that these blessings had been there all along during my tenure decision. I had simply ignored them and chosen to focus on what I didn't have. I had allowed my ego to run the show for too long. Once I shifted my perspective, these baseline blessings led me to much better thoughts and emotions.

Don't misunderstand what I am saying here. I am not telling you to focus on baseline blessings to create an environment of complacency. It isn't to let you off the hook for pursuing your purpose and potential. Instead, it is designed to cultivate a mindset that frees you up completely to pursue your "beyond blessings." These are the dream outcomes that you are passionate about attracting in your life. Once you have a baseline of blessings established, you no longer need to fear falling short of expectations because your brain will already know that you have more than enough. This will free you up to go get your dreams.

DON'T MISS THE POINT...

It would be a huge mistake if I led you to believe that scarcity was reserved only for profound moments when we lose something significant in our lives. Adversity doesn't have a monopoly on the "not enough" mentality. The reality is that scarcity is a common occurrence in our society that impacts pretty much every human being on the planet. It just happens to be far subtler than most people realize. Pretty much daily, most of us scan our environment and subconsciously make comparisons to the people around us. When it doesn't stack up to expectations, it tends to make us feel inadequate because of the perception of where we believe we should be in our lives. Social media has only made this habit of comparing more accessible, immediate and prominent.

It can creep in when we look around at people advancing in their careers and feel like we haven't accomplished enough. *Been there, done that.* The same thing occurs when we see people with lots of really nice things and wish we had those same things in our lives. *Guilty as charged.* It can even pop up as we compare our own kids to others in our day-to-day interactions. *Wish I could say I have never done this!* There are literally thousands of examples just like this that lower our results and quality of life on a daily basis. The fascinating thing is that we often do these things without even knowing it. The patterns are subconscious and happen so quickly that we rarely even know what occurred. We just know that we don't feel like we have enough.

I know what you might be thinking. *Coyte, what if I am comparing to others as a measuring stick to achieve more in my life?* Well, if that's the case and it's being done productively, then by all means go about your business. However, I advise you to be cautious here because this approach can be a slippery slope. I have learned from personal experience that when you get in the habit of comparing to others, it often leads down a path to an undesirable end destination. Before you know it, you might just find yourself invaded by envy, frustration, jealousy, sadness and/or a general sense of not being enough.

It's not worth this risk when you have far more empowering options that will pull out your highest potential.

One more thing about this whole comparison and scarcity thing. I absolutely advise against it, but if you are going to do it, at least give yourself some protection. It isn't fair, reasonable or smart to make these comparisons based on other people's "highlight reels" on social media. Nor does it make sense to judge your self-worth solely on another person's area of giftedness. These rarely give you the entire picture because the reality is that most people have areas of their lives where they are thriving. But the truth is, if you had a chance to look closer, you would find areas where they were falling short of expectations just like you and me. Looking at their highlight clips while ignoring the areas of your life that are special is also another recipe for disappointment.

Maybe none of this is the point though. As I sat in a cozy guest home on the remote island of Atka, Alaska, I couldn't help but gravitate towards the idea of really unique destinations. I was gifted with a rare crystal clear day in the Aleutian Islands and I took full advantage of the breathtaking views all around me. I couldn't help but admire the gorgeous beach landscape that curved outwards around the small village that was the home to 47 Alutiiq people. Glancing up at the snow-capped mountains directly to my left, I had an aha moment that left a lasting impression on my mind.

What if you are destined for a place far more incredible and rewarding than the one you are comparing to right now?

What if using other people as a standard is taking your focus away from a remarkable journey you could be taking in your own life right now at this moment?

Don't rob yourself of the unique opportunity to travel to an extraordinary destination in your life because you become too overly consumed with other people's journeys. That, my friends, is the point. Don't miss it in your own life.

THE SACRIFICES OF SCARCITY

I was sitting in my office one week after my trip to the Aleutian Islands reflecting on this process when I had a breakthrough insight. *Scarcity is never going to get me the results and life I desire.* When I thought about the implications of my current negative habits, I realized that the focus on what I didn't have in my life was robbing me of three things. First, I was literally giving away my power to focus on blessings that would make my life vibrant. The reality was that I had some incredible gifts in my life and all I had to do to feel joyful was to point my brain to them on a consistent basis. Instead, I was choosing miserable emotional states by deciding not to acknowledge them. If this continued, it would only be because I chose to allow it to continue.

Second, I started to realize that every minute I spend on scarcity was a minute I could have allocated to the pursuit of abundance in my life. Each time I brought up my tenure decision with the wrong perspective, I was reinforcing the exact things I wanted to move on from. This was all time that could be dedicated to dreaming up a life that I was passionate about bringing to fruition. Every second of scarcity was a second that could have been generously donated to my hopes and dreams.

Finally, my focus on the past and not enough was subtly stealing my chance to be fully present in my life. Every time I thought about the job I no longer had and what it had cost me, I was giving away an opportunity to make moments with the people who mattered to me most: my family. I was also forfeiting the chance to bring the best of me to my new coaching and speaking business that could grant me a remarkable and memorable future. The point is that I knew that there were clear sacrifices to focusing on scarcity and these were costs that I was not willing to pay anymore. So I doubled down on my baseline blessings when I arrived at a transformational concept that helped me take things to an entirely different level.

SOME OF GOD'S GREATEST GIFTS...

In 1990, country music icon Garth Brook's released a song entitled "Unanswered Prayers" that went on to hit #1 on Billboard's Hot Country Songs chart. In the song, he goes on a journey exploring the disappointing times in his life where he prayed to God to have them turn out better. As the song runs its course, he eloquently illustrates how sometimes life's greatest gifts are the ones when we don't get exactly what we want in the moment. I think anyone can relate to this message regardless of their religious beliefs. Why? Because there are times in all of our lives when these "unanswered prayers" turn into unexpected gifts. This has unequivocally been true in my own life.

There was a time in my life when the only thing in the world I wanted was to win an NCAA Championship in wrestling. I poured my heart into training at a grueling level that would give me the best chance possible to achieve this goal. I gave it everything I had in this demanding sport for five full years to try to bring this dream to fruition. When I fell short my senior year, it was a devastating time for me that hurt for months afterwards. I made All-American, but it didn't seem like enough. I was so disappointed that I had a hard time catching a breath when I woke up each morning and remembered that I didn't achieve my goal.

There was another time in college when I would have done anything to have my then college girlfriend love me. Ultimately, she decided to pursue another option (one of my high school best friends) and I was depressed for months afterwards. There was also a time when I wished I could be tenured at the University of North Carolina. As you are already aware, that didn't happen and I was faced with a wide range of emotions that negatively impacted my life.

These three painful times became my "unanswered prayers." While frustrating in the moment, each of these situations morphed into profound turning points in my life. The disappointment of failing to win an NCAA Championship led me to a decision to walk away from wrestling to pursue my

Ph.D. This afforded me the opportunity to become a professor and to explore my passion of impacting lives in a unique manner as a teacher. The hurt of my college girlfriend ditching me for one of my best friends forced me to walk away from the relationship to reflect on my life. Six months later, with the encouragement of my brother, I decided to start "meeting people" again and mysteriously stumbled upon a gorgeous Midwest girl named Brandy. Now 16 years later, she is my soulmate and the mother of my two incredible children Carter and Mya. Brandy is the center of my world and the single best thing that has ever happened to me.

What's the lesson here? I think you already know. Sometimes the path isn't perfect, but if you keep getting up and looking for the gift, eventually it can lead you to a point better than you ever imagined possible. This can't happen if you stay down and allow scarcity to steal your perspective. You must get back up and commit to consistently pointing your brain to possible. With this perspective point in mind, I decided to see if I could find the hidden gift in my current situation.

SO REALLY..."WHAT'S THE GIFT?"

If I was going to find the gift in my situation, I knew that I needed to train my brain to see things differently. I decided that it made sense to add a new element to my morning "Baseline Blessings" ritual. Right after I had experienced three things I was grateful for in my life, I added a fourth element to flip the script on scarcity. It was pretty simple really. I took the most challenging current situation in my life (losing my job) and asked myself, *What's the gift?* I wanted to see if I could find something good in the middle of something I would have never chosen in a million years.

I have to admit that it didn't work right off the bat. The first time I asked it, my brain intuitively responded, *Nothing dummy. You just got fired from a job you loved. There is no gift in that.* I guess my brain had gotten used to finding scarcity in times of adversity. This had become the standard default for my brain. However, knowing what was now at stake, I refused to accept this as an answer so I kept asking with curiosity until I forced my brain to give me a better option. I knew I had to keep showing up and carve out a new neural pathway to possible in my mind.

What could be the gift from being denied tenure?

After a few weeks, my brain finally started to admit that this might be a prime opportunity to pursue my dream. It was a hesitant response at first, but it intrigued me nonetheless. However, as I kept asking, my belief in this opportunity strengthened until I was excited to embark on my new journey.

I honestly had no idea that this shift would have such a profound impact on my entire life. Once I had taught my brain to find the gift in my most challenging situation, it naturally started to do the same thing with pretty much everything. When simple things like bad weather popped up, I didn't miss a beat because I felt blessed to be able to stay inside and write this book. When more difficult things like losing a $30,000 branding contract presented itself, I immediately redirected my brain within minutes to the opportunity to create new and better products in my true passion zone.

I started to realize that this one simple cue had trained my brain to find productive in virtually any situation I was facing. It turns out that the actual question was really the gift because it gave me a tool to control my happiness, productivity and ability to close the gap on the results and life I desired. It blew me away that you could make such a radical shift in your life by simply intentionally programming your brain with the right focal points. This wasn't just a gift for me. It unlocked my ability to DELIVER a gift – the ability to lead others down a similar path.

I truly felt empathy for one of my mentees who was going through a painful divorce and was experiencing sadness about the loss in her life. But I also knew that I wouldn't serve her one bit by sitting and being an accomplice to a pity party. So I urged her to ask herself, *what is the gift in this situation?* She eventually realized that her previous husband was completely wrong for her and started to invest in a value system that would build her up. She began to work her morning growth routine like a champ. About a year later, this special woman met an incredible man who was a perfect fit for her. All because she was willing to seek out the gift in the most challenging situation in her life.

There are so many applications to this philosophy. If you failed to reach a goal that truly mattered to you, maybe this is the time to seek a new path with the potential to lead you to your true purpose in life. If you are having financial struggles, this might be the exact situation you needed to make an adamant decision that your career will stand for something different moving forward. If you don't believe me, then study some of the most successful people on the planet. You will learn that pain is often the pathway to purpose for incredible people like Bill Gates, Ellen DeGeneres, J.K. Rowling, Oprah Winfrey and Russell Wilson.

THE GREATEST GIFT I COULD GIVE YOU...

With all this talk of gifts, I feel like it is time for me to give one to you. If I could wave a magic wand right now and deliver you any one single gift, it would be a growth system. I know you are probably disappointed that I didn't choose a million dollars, but this one is actually much better. Just trust me. I would choose this because a powerful growth system can lead you to virtually any result that you desire in life. In the process, it also allows you to EARN the ability to control your emotions and that is priceless.

I wouldn't just give you any old growth system though. I know better than to be careless about the activities to include because not all habits are created equally. I would only include the ones that would help you breakthrough your biggest barriers. In this package would be world-class habits designed to pull out your passion, purpose and potential. Each one would be carefully picked to build on top of each other so they would compound and help you create a life you absolutely love.

I know you are dying to find out exactly what I would include in your package. The first gift would be a love for rising early. For just a brief moment, I could know what it felt like to be "Coyt-y Claus" on Christmas morning as I carefully delivered you an ability to jump out of bed at 5:00am with a passion to pursue your highest potential. No more hitting the snooze button and dreading having to leave the comfort of your cozy bed. Instead, you would have the "Sacred Space" you need and deserve to invest in yourself. There are few things more precious than filling your tank and this would be your own special time to make that happen.

The second gift I would give you would be a deep love for growth and diving into profound books that inspire you and help you tap into your highest potential. Inside this box would be a never-ending curiosity that drives you to read voraciously so you are able to break down barriers and get in touch with your talents. This would be a gift that would continue to give for the rest of your life because it would help you fill your mind with productive thoughts and eventually put you on the path to your purpose.

My plan is to continue to give you life altering gifts throughout the rest of this book. But for now I am going to stop at three because that seems like a nice round number for a pleasant gift package. Any more than that might seem boastful. I don't want to be the guy who comes across as a showoff because I overdid it with my present. Besides, I can't give you all of them right now because then you would have no incentive to keep reading. How about I sprinkle in one more for now and build a little suspense? Without further ado, I present you your final gift in this life altering growth package: *gratitude*.

At first glance, it might seem like an underwhelming gift to receive, but don't be fooled. On the inside of this wrapping paper is one of the single most influential shifts you can implement to transform your life. It will provide you with the ability to control your response to any situation that life sends your way. It will allow you to focus on blessings that make your life vibrant right now. It will build up your ability to channel your inner Viktor Frankl so you can always take the lemons in life and turn them into lemonade. It is the opportunity to feel truly blessed to have the chance to live this life.

FLIPPIN SCARCITY

What was the turning point in my tenure situation? The moment I got sick and tired of scarcity! I was completely over focusing on what I didn't have because I knew the cost. I was no longer willing to settle for the flippin status quo in my life. Once I made this decision, the solution to my scarcity mindset revealed itself. I simply had to give my brain a better option by getting up each morning and reminding myself of the specific things I was blessed to have in my life. This immediately started to quiet scarcity and improved my attitude. It was at this point that I realized that my focus was something that I could completely control with the right programming and approach.

If scarcity is currently present in your approach, I hope you are sick of it. If there is one thing I have learned from my journey, it is that focusing on not enough will never allow you to tap into your highest potential. It will never allow you to grab onto those gifts inside of you that are meant to help you achieve remarkable things in your life. The game changing mental shift here is to remind yourself that there is more than enough in this world for you to achieve your desired outcomes in life. If this thought process sounds intriguing to you, then it's time to flip the script on scarcity. Decide right now to be done with any belief system that leads you to believe that there is not enough. In their place, let's start to establish an attitude of gratitude that leads you to abundance.

YELLOW BALL #2
THE "BLESSED BANK" HABIT

It actually turns out that I can't hand you the habit of gratitude. That isn't really bad though because it will mean so much more when you EARN it. I will simply provide you with the framework so you can go out and cultivate an "ever abundant" attitude of gratitude. All you have to do to start making this happen is show up and build your "Blessed Bank." This means showing up each morning in your growth routine and writing down the "Baseline Blessings" we discussed in the chapter. Simply get a journal to dedicate solely to the activities outlined in this book and write down three blessings you have in your life that you are truly grateful for. Don't mail it in here. Instead, commit to really feeling each of these things so you create an emotion response that grabs your brain's attention. Then add the fourth powerful element where you take your most challenging situation and ask yourself with curiosity, *what's the gift?* Keep asking until you have an option you are truly excited about. That's it! Welcome to your second yellow ball. Commit to the "Blessed Bank" for the next 66-days and flip the script on scarcity in your life once and for all.

"

SOMETIMES THE PATH ISN'T PERFECT,
BUT IF YOU KEEP GETTING UP AND

LOOKING FOR **THE GIFT**

EVENTUALLY IT CAN LEAD YOU TO A POINT

BETTER THAN YOU EVER IMAGINED POSSIBLE

CHAPTER 3

NOT ENOUGH

VAULT YOUR LIFE VIA VISION BLUEPRINTING

"Keep your thoughts positive because your thoughts become your words. Keep your words positive because your words become your behaviors. Keep your behaviors positive because your behavior becomes your habits. Keep your habits positive because your habits become your values. Keep your values positive because your values become your destiny."

—Mahatma Gandhi

It was a beautiful Spring morning in the San Juan Islands. My wife and I were celebrating our 12th Anniversary and the kids had gone over to grandma and grandpa's house for the weekend. Brandy had to take a shower to get ready so I decided to take my Siberian Husky Kira on a run. We hit the trails and I was immediately mesmerized by all the beauty around me that is the norm in the Pacific Northwest. I decided to shift my music to Journey's Greatest Hits on my iPhone and this instantaneously took me back 15 years. I thought about how blessed I was to meet Brandy and just how much that changed the course of my entire life. I absolutely LOVED our family and felt an overwhelming sense of gratitude reminiscing on it all. I was totally immersed in these emotions when I felt an out-of-the-blue urge to look up. My eyes immediately locked in on an incredible heart-shaped rock in the middle of the trail. I knew right away that

I needed to pick it up and take it with me. As I admired it while running home, it occurred to me that I had just landed upon a special lesson that radically changed my entire perspective.

Listen, I know what you might be thinking. *Grea-a-a-a-t, you found a rock! Congrats Coyte! What do you want...a cookie for your efforts or a golden star? What does this have to do with me?* I promise I didn't just tell this story to fill space. It might not seem all that profound right now, but it will once I give you a little context and you connect how it relates to your own life. You see, when I found that rock, love had been an intentional point of emphasis in my life. I had been urging myself daily to seek it out and to make sure I was expressing it to the most important people around me. I had heard the message reinforced from my pastor Ken Hubbard, read about it in books and emphasized it consistently in my daily morning growth routine. On top of this, I was completely in a loving state given that it was my anniversary. I had intentionally flooded my brain with love so that it was a priority in my approach.

When you start to add all of this to the equation, it actually becomes pretty remarkable that my subconscious brain found that one single heart-shaped rock on a trail that was the home to literally thousands of rocks. *Oh, yeah, did I mention that my wife loves and collects heart-shaped rocks?* When you start to take all of this into account, it makes you realize how incredible our brain's capacity is to find the exact things we need when we program it based on our highest values. Without knowing it, I had trained my brain to find love in my surrounding environment. This concept has been reinforced dozens of times when I go to a beach and instinctively find the perfect heart-shaped rock without any intentional effort.

Wouldn't it be nice if this was the way our brain operated all the time? It would just cruise on out into the world each day and instinctively find the exact things we needed with ease. It seems to be too good to be true. What if I told you that our brain actually *does* have this capacity? With the right inputs, it has more than enough bandwidth to seek out and find the path to the outcomes you desire. If that's true, you might be thinking, *then why is it that so many people seem to be stuck with results and lives so far below their hopes and expectations*? It all comes down to the fact that most of us have unknowingly programmed our brains with negative focal points that drag on our potential. It turns out that our brain's unlimited capacity is just as good at seeking out and finding junk if that is what it has been instructed to do.

This is exactly what I had initially done following my UNC situation. We have outlined my focus on scarcity in the previous chapter, but it turns out that there was more to it than that for me. It wasn't just about the things I no longer had in my life. I was also focused on the things I was not. *I'm not a respected professor. I'm not a faculty member at one of the best universities in the United States.* This was leading me to thoughts, emotions and pictures that filled my brain with disappointment. I knew that I needed to give my mind a better option if I was going to flip the script on not enough once and for all.

REFLECT, RECOGNIZE AND REDIRECT

Over and over again, I have seen a similar pattern in clients that I have worked with in a coaching capacity. As humans, we seem to be very effective at scanning our environment and comparing ourselves to others. Naturally, when we are focusing on what we are not, this gives us emotions that are far less than ideal. Frustration, disappointment and sadness come to mind. My initial yellow ball habits had taught me that I could train my brain to flip the script on these negative patterns. I was ready to create another new alternative to not enough that would empower my potential. This is when I connected three unique steps that would help me flip the script on any counterproductive habit moving forward: *reflect, recognize* and *redirect*.

The first step involves a reflection process. If you are going to flip the feeling of not being enough as a human being, the initial thing you need to do is gain an awareness of the instances when you are focusing on your limitations. For me, this generally included moments when I replayed the fact that I had my dream career position taken from me. This would only repeatedly lead me to questioning whether I was enough. It wasn't productive and I now knew that. I had reflected and advanced to the second phase in this process.

Most of the time, we don't even recognize the instances when we are focused on disempowering thoughts that drag on our potential. Life gets so cluttered that we rarely slow down enough to consider how our chosen mindset is attracting emotions and results we don't want. Once I reflected, I started to recognize specific thoughts and beliefs that were flat out not serving me one bit. This was a breakthrough for me because I began to notice behaviors that I could flip to increase my productivity and potential. This led me to the final phase of this new in-the-moment flip the script strategy.

Before we move on to the final phase in the process, I want to point out a powerful barrier that commonly stops people from flipping the script on their worst habits. Whenever people reflect on their performance, they inevitably stumble upon another "R" outcome: *realization*. They realize that their behavior has cost them significant time and precious moments in the past. I always remind myself that this is an instance when you EARN the next level in your life. Rather than dwelling on disappointment, you need to create a new habit where you point your brain to opportunity. Actively seek out the chance you have to create a new empowering option for your brain that will free you up and allow you to CRUSH IT in your life moving forward. Now that we have that out of the way, we are ready to move onto the final step in this process.

The final step in flipping the script on not enough is giving your brain a better, more empowering option. Rather than focusing on all the ways you perceive yourself as not being enough as a human being, why not try a kinder approach? One thing that helped me was redirecting to three things that I knew to be true about myself that I absolutely loved.

I show up for things that matter to me.

I inspire people to live better in their lives.

I am a loving father and husband.

Then I identified five values that I was passionate about pursuing and started to program them into my brain every single day. This gave me a set of incredible focal points to redirect to every single time I found myself noticing not enough. It was around this time that I found a quirky strategy that took this flip the script process to a completely different stratosphere.

THE SCIENTIFIC SH-H-H-H-H METHOD

I was sitting in my office one day chugging away at writing this book. Things were flowing nicely and I got to the point when I finished the draft of my final chapter. I was so excited about the progress that I got up and started clapping my hands in celebration. It was a milestone moment and that was an amazing feeling. It was about this time that a doubt snuck into my brain unexpectedly.

But what if it falls short?

What if what you have done here is not enough?

There was a time when I may have overresponded to this voice in my head, but not this time. Instead, I came up with one of the coolest methods out of the blue that silenced this self-doubting inner critic. It turns out that this quirky, outside-the-box method was actually backed by science.

Wait, who am I kidding? There is nothing scientific about this approach. Well, at least nothing specific I know about that backs it up. But I know for sure that it has worked remarkably well for me and my clients the past couple years. Are you ready for it? All right, here it is. On that day when my inner critic creeped in to cast doubt on my progress, I noticed it immediately, but decided not to respond to it in a normal manner. Instead, I simply made a #1 sign with my finger, promptly put it up to my lips and proceeded to make a "s-h-h-h-h" sound. I then confidently said to myself, *Yeah, I don't need you anymore. It's time for you to go somewhere else.*

I honestly don't know exactly what prompted me to do this. I just had the urge to do it and followed my intuition. That was the boost I needed to anchor my new "reflect, recognize and redirect" approach. The moment I did the "s-h-h-h-h" strategy, it created a signal to my brain that I was now ready for a better option.

It also served one other purpose for me. When I first did it, it was so different that it made me smile. I quickly learned that this was a powerful pattern interrupt because it put me into a happier state. This made my process so much stronger because happiness lent itself extremely well to my new conditioning.

If you are going to flip the script on not enough, it's important that you start to create a simple process that allows you to redirect counterproductive thoughts and beliefs. Now that you know how to interrupt and redirect them, it is time to move on to creating a better, more empowering option for your mind. It's critical that we find focal points that are so intriguing that they demand your brain's full attention. This is what it will take to overcome the crazy clutter that is present all around us every single day. We need to give our mind something to focus on that triggers empowering emotions that drive productive behaviors moving forward.

THE FUNERAL EXERCISE

You already know that one of my biggest struggles during my journey was breaking free from the pattern of focusing on what I was not. I had gotten into the habit of reminding myself daily that I had not gotten tenure at UNC. I also kept retelling my brain that I was no longer an Assistant Professor at one of the best public institutions in the United States.

Sh-h-h-h-h-h, it's time to go away not enough.

We don't need you anymore.

The truth is that this focus was only going to bring me more pain and disappointment. I didn't want to experience either one of these emotions so it was time to step up and give my brain a better option. It was right around this time that I remembered a powerful exercise I had experienced while a doctoral student at Indiana University.

I was grinding away on page 150 of my doctoral dissertation on my old school, boxy Dell computer station when I hit a wall. I was tapped out. I was completely over calculating data so I rose from my chair and started pacing around my office. Being a former wrestler, I started bouncing around the room while vigorously shaking my arms out repeatedly at my sides. Hoping that it would bring me back to life, I slapped my face lightly three times with both of my hands before returning to my work station to continue my process. *Nope, still tapped out,* I thought to myself. *I'll take another 15-minutes off and see if that doesn't do the trick.* So I decided to do something that I wish could say was more meaningful. I got on Facebook and scrolled my timeline to take my mind off of work. In hindsight, I realize I got lucky this time.

I had only checked out a couple of updates when I stumbled upon a video by the legendary thought leader Dr. Stephen Covey. I immediately hit the play button and realized that he was doing a keynote talk on legacy and how to live a life that leaves a lasting impression on others. He paused for a moment on stage before asking the audience to close their eyes. *Heck, I don't want to return to my dissertation yet,* I thought to myself. *Might as well give it a shot.* Dr. Covey strolled to the other side of the stage as he promptly gave instructions I will never forget. He proceeded to ask the audience to imagine themselves at their own funeral with the most important people in their life in attendance. This immediately piqued my interest as nobody had ever asked me to do anything quite like this before in my life.

I was dutifully imagining all of the details of the funeral room when Dr. Covey gave us the next instruction. "I want you to imagine three of the most important people in your life coming to the front of the room to say a few words about you," he explained. "But here is the kicker. It can't be what you want them to say. It has to be what they would say if they were being 100 percent honest and had to give the pros and cons about your life." I paused for a moment to ponder this as two words immediately emerged in my mind: *Oh shit!* I realized immediately that I was not living anywhere near the level I desired in the key areas of my life.

It wasn't that I was doing terrible. I was quite certain that the people close to me would say some really nice things about me. The problem was that they would also have some less than ideal things to express if they were being completely honest in their funeral speeches. If my fiancé at the time Brandy was being candid, I think she would have likely said that I was a good guy who loved her and treated her well most of the time. But I also believe that she would have said that I was a flippin jerk at times. She would have proceeded to outline moments when I was impatient and a tad annoying. Honestly, she would have been completely justified in saying that. It was a fair assessment!

The one thing that really struck me is that she wouldn't have been able to say that I did everything in my power to make her life special and to help her live to her highest potential. I knew right away that this wasn't all right with me. Rather than dwell on what I was not, I immediately pointed my brain to a powerful question that allowed me to reflect on the person I was passionate about becoming in my own life.

How do you want the most important people in your life to remember you?

I instantly realized that there were undeniably things I wanted to become for the people I loved most in my life. It was time to own my legacy. So I did what made sense to me at the time. I took out a piece of paper and started writing down exactly what I would want Brandy to say about me someday at my funeral.

Coyte was an incredible husband who loved me unconditionally every single day. There was not a single day that passed where he did not show me how important I was to him. He was incredibly kind, remarkably patient and unbelievably supportive on a daily basis. Coyte believed in me more than anybody else has in my life and always did things to help me be the best version of myself. I couldn't have asked for a better partner to do life with! I feel so blessed to have had him as a soulmate and the father of our children!

This immediately sparked a powerful passion deep inside of me. I wasn't a parent yet, but I felt the urge to do the same thing for my future role as a father. I have since done it as a professional as well. This built my desire to control my daily approach to living even more. It was this process, which I now call vision blueprinting, that made me realize that I never want to settle for status quo in the areas of life that matter to me most. I didn't want my wife, kids and clients to say I was just all right. I wanted them to say that I showed up with passion and added CRAZY VALUE to their lives every single day. I had officially stumbled upon a value vision process that would drive profound change in my life in the future.

BRINGING BACK THE VISION BLUEPRINT

Everyone has times in life when they fall short. This can be disappointing. But what if it doesn't have to be? What if those moments when we didn't meet expectations were just building up to something bigger? I started to suspect that this was potentially the case in my own life. It was not my intention, but I had slowly moved away from the vision blueprint process that had made a profound impact on my life. It would be easy to look back and see this as a missed opportunity. Instead, I leaned on my core belief that sometimes we learn lessons along the way in life that are designed to be a part of our overall bigger journey. I had unintentionally fallen short on this process, but it was something that I had learned that could contribute to helping me flip the script on my current limiting beliefs.

As I reflected on past times when my life was truly vibrant, I fondly remembered the experience of going through the funeral exercise. *What was it about this activity that made it so impactful?* I pondered. Within minutes the answer was crystal clear. I had given my brain an incredibly powerful vision to pursue in the areas of life that were most important to me. *Bingo!* I concluded. *That is EXACTLY what I need to do in my life right now! I need to stop focusing on not enough and instead give my brain an outcome to pursue that is more than enough!* I immediately decided that this was the ideal next habit to layer into my morning growth routine.

Before adding the vision blueprint outcomes to my ritual, I knew I needed to move through the process to freshen it up. It had been over seven years since I created my initial value visions and I was at a completely different place in my life. The first thing I did was sit down and brainstorm the areas of my life that I valued most. I was looking for the roles that I was deeply passionate about being extraordinary in. It only took me a few minutes to confirm that *family* and *career* were my two clear top values. These were areas that I was ready to pour my heart and soul into every single day. The remaining three values took a little more time because there were several options worthy of consideration. After some serious reflection, I settled on *vitality, growth* and *faith* as my final three value areas. It was officially time to move on to the vision portion of the process.

I settled in at my desk to begin the blueprint process. It was time to find the outcomes I was passionate about pursuing in these value areas. I got out my yellow notepad and wrote "#1" and "Family" at the top of the page. Then I started to write down the outcomes I was passionate about pursuing in my family moving forward. I quickly realized that I needed a process to narrow my focus so I wasn't completely overwhelmed by my options. I eventually came up with a simple criteria that ensured that I was choosing outcomes that were worthy of my time, ENERGY and full attention. I basically had three core criteria I needed to meet to include an outcome in my vision blueprint. I used this when brainstorming in each of my top five value areas.

1. **The ENERGIZE Criteria:** The outcome must create an emotional response that excites me when I think about it.

2. **The "Fight For It" Criteria:** The outcome is something that is important enough that I am willing to fight for it each day even when I don't feel like it.

3. **The Happiness Criteria:** The outcome is something that will likely bring me sustainable happiness in my life.

I basically gave myself a 5-minute period in each value area to brainstorm outcomes that I was passionate about. At the end of these sessions, I used my criteria to make sure that each outcome was worthy of my time and would allow me to thrive in my life moving forward. By the time I finished this process, I had blueprints in each value area with 3-4 desirable outcomes that charged me up. I was so excited to get out and start bringing them to fruition. It was time to move on to the programming process.

THE BLUEPRINT PROGRAMMING PROCESS

It's such an invigorating experience to write down a vision that inspires you to live to potential in your top value areas. When combining this with a quieting of your inner critic, this becomes a progression that pulls out passion that was previously lying dormant inside of you. There is something so magical and transformational about dreaming of a life so powerful that it urges you to take on your biggest barriers. Once you have some initial outcomes that you are willing to fight for, you have a solid shot of creating meaningful change in your life. This is when you need to maximize your chances of success by getting to work with the programming process.

What exactly is the programming process? It is the part where you take the outcomes you are crazy passionate about and intentionally program them into your subconscious brain. This is actually a simpler process than you might anticipate. Don't misunderstand me here because it is difficult to show up and fight for the things that matter to you most in a cluttered world. It just means that the process of training your brain to pursue the things you love is initially pretty straight forward. It is accomplished by being disciplined enough to expose your mind to your value visions every single day. This is a prerequisite to form a new neural pathway in your brain that drives intentional behaviors towards the outcomes you desire.

I started to get up every single morning and revisited my value visions with a passion. I knew I had to drum up emotion when doing it to grab my brain's attention and remind it that these were top priorities in my life. It turns out that this wasn't an easy task to accomplish because there were days when my ENERGY and focus waned. It was in these times that I reminded myself to show up and fight for the outcomes I desired in my life. *It doesn't make a difference if you don't feel like it or not. These are YOUR dreams and they are worth fighting for.* I knew I had to EARN my highest aspirations.

It didn't take me long to recognize that emotion was the key ingredient to driving productive behavior in my life. When I drummed up emotion for my value visions, my brain got more engaged in the process and built momentum in my days. However, there were also days when I struggled to emotionally connect with them. I had to remind myself that anyone can show up and follow through on their intentions when it's easy. It's in the moments when motivation wanes that you have the greatest opportunities to close the gap on your biggest goals. I quickly learned that being able to drum up real emotion for your dreams in challenging environments is a master skill set.

DON'T MAIL IT IN

I had to really stretch my creative capacity to find unique ways to drum up emotion for my dreams on a consistent basis. If you saw me going through the latter half of my morning routine, there is a good chance you would think I was a little insane. It isn't at all uncommon to find me bouncing around, clapping my hands vigorously, raising my hands towards the sky and/or dancing around my office to music. It's safe to say that most people don't generally do this stuff at all, let alone at 5:00am when most of the rest of the world is soundly asleep. I do it because I know I must to be willing to fight for my value visions. There is no doubt in my mind that emotion is the key to making sure my brain is on board to bring my dreams to fruition. I can't ever mail that in.

A fascinating thing happened as I continued to show up and find new ways to emotionally connect to my value visions. Every day I followed through and found my "WHY," my intention and passion for the life I desired grew exponentially. It was about more than just training my brain to get results that would make my life vibrant. I realized that this was the key to giving my mind an empowering option that would drown out negativity. It was in the middle of this programming process that I truly learned how to flip the script on not enough. I had taken another step to redirect my brain from problems to possible.

As we wrap this chapter up, I need to make one last plea to you. Don't mail it in! It can be so easy to neglect this process as you implement it into your morning routine. The moment you coast and go through the motions, the activity becomes mundane and your brain will tune you out. It will think *WAMP-WAMP* and go find a "better" dopamine hit on your mobile device. This might be one of the single most important concepts to grab when striving to flip the script in your life. There are thousands of strategies out there on ways to change your life. You learned a powerful one in this chapter. While this is a really good thing, it will mean nothing if you mail it in and see it as an obligation. The moment you learn to drum up emotion and see it as an opportunity, it will transform the experience into magical moments that lead your life to an incredible place.

FIND YOUR HEART ROCK

At the beginning of the chapter, I led with a story about how I unexpectedly found a single heart rock for my wife Brandy on our Anniversary while running on a trail littered with thousands of rocks. The fascinating thing is that I never initially set out to find something that would make Brandy's day special. I was just going to enjoy a run with my Husky pup while she took a shower. However, I had been focusing extensively on love in my morning routine and daily approach. This had subconsciously trained my brain to look for ways to show love to the most important people in my life. It's clear to me after the fact that it was simply responding to the programming I had given it. That is the power that each of us has when we give our brain a powerful blueprint to carry out.

It's time to find your heart rock. No, I don't really literally mean going out and finding a heart rock to prove that you can. It's probably not productive for you and it wouldn't work anyways if it isn't something you are passionate about. What I'm talking about here is showing up every single day and training your brain to seek out your value visions. Don't allow yourself to fall into the trap that millions of people do when they wake up and live by default. This leads to negative programming patterns that create a drag on your life. You are capable of so much more if you are bold enough to step up and intentionally point your brain to inspiring dreams that will make your life dynamic and vibrant.

You honestly don't have to wrap your brain around the entire vision blueprint process at this point. The only thing that is required to start is that you identify some desirable outcomes that spark intrigue in your soul. This may sound complicated, but it really just involves finding things that matter to you deeply enough that you will fight for them. If you show up with excitement and point your brain to these visions on a consistent daily basis, you will program your brain to find ways to close the gap on them. It doesn't have to be complicated. Just silence your inner critic and point your mind to things that empower your potential. Do it over and over even if you don't feel like it.

Disappointment is a part of life. When I got denied tenure, it was a natural instinct to focus on what I had lost. Our brain is wired to keep us safe so it makes sense that it locked in on the things that had hurt me. I learned two valuable lessons during this part of my journey. First, focusing on what I wasn't would never lead me to the outcomes that I desired in life. It was only going to lead to more reasons to justify why I wasn't enough. Second, I realized that this was a response that was completely within my control. I could flip the script on my "not enough as a human being" focus by giving my brain a much better option. It turns out that this was possible by showing up every single day and passionately reinforcing to my brain the life I wanted to be living.

As we wrap up this chapter, I want to urge you to remind yourself that there are few things more empowering in life than training your brain to pursue your dreams. I truly believe that this is a critical step that will serve as a foundational block to flip the script on your biggest barriers in life. When you have something powerful that you are willing to fight for, it gives you a focal point worthy of your brain's full attention. I know you still have it in you to dream up things you are passionate about achieving in your life. Everyone still has that creative, limitless inner child somewhere deep inside of them. If you keep showing up and asking yourself with curiosity what you would love your life to look like in your top value areas, eventually a vision will start to emerge.

Once the vision starts to unveil itself, simply show up and drum up emotion for your dreams on a consistent daily basis. When that silent inner critic shows up to try to talk you down, simply put your number one finger up to your lips and say, "Sh-h-h-h-h." Then point your brain directly to the life that you desire and celebrate the fact that you just cast a vote for your highest potential. Keep pointing your brain to the life you plan to be living in the future with excitement until it comes to fruition.

FLIPPIN NOT ENOUGH

Do you know one of the most valuable lessons I learned during the latter part of my journey. *Change can be accelerated.* That is, if you get your mind in a higher-level state as you start to implement a new, life altering habit. My biggest changes came when I made a simple, profound decision that I was completely finished with my old, useless counterproductive habits. I was sick of them so there was no discussion needed. It was non-negotiable. At this point, I knew that all I needed to do was give my brain a better option that would bring it pleasure. That is where my value visions came into play.

Now to the part on accelerating the process. The moment you choose something that is backed by passion, it accelerates the process. Why? Because your brain responds really well to charged positive emotions. But don't be fooled here because seeing your inspiring value visions once will never do the trick. Instead, you have to show up on a consistent daily basis and bring passion to your process. Even when you don't feel it, you need to find new ways to tap into your emotions because it is necessary to maintain your brain's attention in a busy cluttered world. Once you do, it will super charge your process because your brain will prioritize the things that bring it pleasure.

I hope you sense the opportunity that is in front of you at this exact moment. Imagine what your life would be like if you flipped the script on not enough once and for all. What would you be able to achieve if you never gave limiting beliefs a chance to take root? It's time to decide that you are done dwelling on not enough. Decide right at this moment that you are capable of giving your brain a better option. Decide that you would rather fight for the things that matter to you than ever settle for the status quo. If you don't mind, just do one more thing for me. Decide that you will commit to chasing this next yellow ball for the next 66-days so you can experience what it is like to start living with supreme passion in your life.

YELLOW BALL #3:

THE "VALUE VISION" HABIT

I think you already have an idea of where we are going here. No need to get fancy. It's time to sit down and do some vision blueprinting. I have a feeling that you will enjoy the simplicity of this process. Find a quiet place where you think best and write down three prioritized values in your life that are most important to you. These should be areas that you have a passion to be extraordinary in moving forward. Once you have these in place, get a sheet of paper for your top value and set a timer for 5-minutes. Remind yourself that there is one rule for the session: *no limiting beliefs during this time frame.*

Once you hit start on your timer, brainstorm any outcomes that come to mind that spark your interest. The important thing here is that you get excited when you think about them. This will help you kickstart your dreamstorming session. When the timer is finished, go back through your list and make sure they meet the (1) ENERGIZE, (2) Fight For It and (3) Sustained Happiness criteria to maximize your chances of success moving forward. If done properly, this should give you a list of outcomes to include in your programming.

Once you have some initial outcomes in place that intrigue you, commit to revisiting your value visions every single day during your morning routine with emotion. Don't be afraid to get a little funky because it will accelerate your habit formation process. Beyond this, all you need to do is continue to be excited for the incredible change you are creating each day under the surface as you chase your yellow ball habits. With each repetition, you are training your brain to focus on positive and are pulling out your potential.

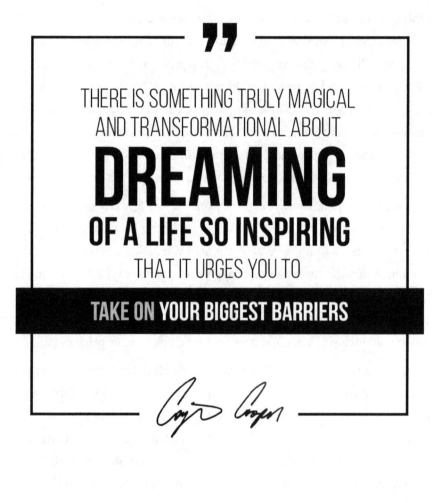

THERE IS SOMETHING TRULY MAGICAL
AND TRANSFORMATIONAL ABOUT

DREAMING

OF A LIFE SO INSPIRING

THAT IT URGES YOU TO

TAKE ON YOUR BIGGEST BARRIERS

CHAPTER 4

INSTANT

NOT EASY, EARN IT

"I've learned over the years that when it comes to success, consistency is key.
Consistent hard work that we may not like doing today,
but for a payoff we will love tomorrow.
Earn it. Enjoy it."

—Dwayne "The Rock" Johnson

I knew exactly what I wanted. I had seen it in my head dozens of times while dancing around my house listening to "Best Day of My Life" by the American Authors. It was so real to me that I could literally see and feel thousands of people jumping around the arena all charged up to create change in their lives. I would get a jolt of ENERGY throughout my entire body every time I visualized the MASSIVE sea of audience members embracing messages that helped them achieve their dreams. I mean goosebumps all over your skin can't lie, right? I would get so amped up visualizing this that I wanted to sprint out of my house at that exact moment and go run the event. Like right now! Then the song would end and I would come back from my "dream sessions" to reality. It was time to take action and bring my dream to fruition. The problem was that I hit a wall when it actually came time to send out invites for my first live event. It seems I was stuck before I even got started.

I had the visualization part down pat. I was starting to be able to see all of my value visions in my mind and that charged me up. I'm sure you can relate. Every person at some point has visualized a desirable outcome in their mind with such clarity and power that it feels totally real. When I started to experience this regularly, it gave me a jolt of inspiration to get out and make my dreams happen. I quickly learned that it's one thing to see a dream you are passionate about pursuing play out in your mind in the safety of your own home. It's another thing entirely to actually get out and take the action necessary to bring it to fruition.

I knew exactly what I wanted, but I was stalling to take the action necessary to close the gap on the outcomes I desired. It took me a few weeks to diagnose the problem. Eventually I noticed that every time I ran up to a barrier, I would start to question why I was not getting the results I desired. *Maybe the dream just isn't right,* I thought to myself. I quickly brushed this off because I knew that running events was something I was passionate about and meant to be doing. This is when an intriguing insight hit me.

The dream is good.

It is my expectations that are causing me to run into a brick wall.

Here is what I eventually realized. Without knowing it, I had created a belief in my mind for when and how my dream had to come to fruition. For now, we will focus on the when part in this chapter. I had fallen into the instant gratification mindset. I had a desire to perform in front of thousands of people at a world-class level, but I wanted it right now. The dream was completely reasonable, but my expectation of the journey and what it would take was not. I knew it was time for a massive shift in my programming if I wanted to experience the next level in my career and life.

The truth is that this was a philosophy that had started to infiltrate all areas of my life. I wanted an annual schedule jam packed with lucrative keynote talks, but I wanted them by the end of the month. I wanted to become a *NY*

Times bestselling author right away. I wanted a dynamic coaching club with thousands of proactive, passionate people within a few months. None of the outcomes were the problem because they were solid. That wasn't the issue. The issue was that I had started to hope they were going to show up instantly with very little struggle.

I knew immediately that I had not earned this right. The reality is that I would have eventually failed if they were handed to me because I would not have known what it took to make them happen. On top of this, I would have taken them for granted because I had not actually worked for them. I had not put in the time and ENERGY to actually deserve these outcomes. It was time for a radical shift in my mindset and expectations.

I reminded myself that the most rewarding accomplishments I had ever experienced in life came through extended periods of discipline, grit and all out effort. They had never been handed to me. Not the state and national championships. Not the Ph.D. degree. Not the TEDx talk. Not the special relationships with my wife and kids. Instead, I had committed to showing up every single day to pursue my goal even when I didn't feel like it.

I quickly realized that I wasn't alone here. Pretty much every single one of the coolest accomplishments on the planet followed this same trend. It turns out that there is a very specific pre-requisite to achieving anything extraordinary. I was never going to get anywhere great with an instant gratification mentality. It was time to flip the script on easy so I could EARN the next level in my life.

THE INCESSANT BARRAGE OF INSTANT

I want to be clear that I never once sat down and made an intentional decision to actually value instant.

There's not a reasonable person on the planet who would ever do that. I didn't sit down one gloomy afternoon and think to myself, *Yeah, that instant gratification approach sure seems reasonable. I think I'll just start expecting easy and see how it plays out for me.* It's completely ridiculous to even read this statement, right? We would never do that. Yet I had somehow subconsciously and unknowingly adopted a belief where I thought my goals and dreams would show up at my doorstep in the next week.

Before you start judging, understand that these beliefs can be extremely subtle. They often work under the surface undermining our efforts to get the results and life we desire. Here's the thing. I'm not alone here. I have worked with thousands of people in a performance capacity and most people have fallen into the same trap. It doesn't take much reflection and observation to realize that the instant gratification expectation has actually become crazy common in our society.

It really isn't all that surprising that this has become a common trend when you think about it. Every single day, we are greeted with an incessant barrage of instant on our technological devices.

Want some entertainment? Switch on your television and find hundreds of channels ready to deliver mindless hours of diversion!

Need something tasty to eat right away? Just cruise on over to your favorite fast food restaurant and have your meal ready in five minutes or less. Or your money back guaranteed!

Health not so great? First off, it may have to do with that fast food habit, but no worries because there are pills for that!

Finances less than desirable? No problem. Just cruise on over to a local convenient store and pick up your lottery ticket. It might be your lucky day!

The point is that we have instant "solutions" to our boredom and problems accessible at all times. People are constantly trying to sell us products that will make our lives easier. With all these promises of instant all around us, it would honestly be more surprising to find large pockets of people fully committed to pursuing their dreams all out. I say this and we haven't even touched on the true toll of technology on our lives. Every single day, most of us are being robbed of our ability to achieve remarkable things and we don't even know it.

THE TOLL OF TECHNOLOGY

We now live in a society where we are led to believe that we have everything we need at our fingertips. We can order the exact thing we want from Amazon and have it by the next day without moving from our couch. We can go to social media at any moment and find "entertainment" that will keep our minds occupied. We can go to our favorite sites and find pretty much any content we desire right away.

If that isn't enough, we can now stream exclusive television shows and movies from our mobile devices in most places on the planet. Just so you know, I am on the remote island of Akta, Alaska way down the Aleutian Islands as I am writing this paragraph, and I am pretty much able to do all of these things. None of this, by the way, is productive when you are writing a book. Yes, I am going to turn off my wireless now so we can get down to business.

We can literally find something at any moment to fulfill our brain's desire for pleasure. It has never been easier to get a dopamine hit. On the surface, it seems rather harmless. Honestly, it comes across as downright convenient. When you are bored (which our brain hates), you can just simply get on your phone and find something mindless to make your unwanted feelings go away. Don't be fooled because there are some seriously harmful consequences to this seemingly, never-ending convenience. There are far too many to outline in this chapter, but I will give you a few to set the tone so we have a shot at flipping the script on instant moving forward.

Neglecting the Precious Present. This might be the single most impactful consequence of allowing technology to dictate the pace in our lives. Everything about technology is instant. It has an addictive way of constantly demanding our attention and driving our behaviors on a daily basis. Before we know it, we literally spend hours scrolling social media trying to find content that satisfies our needs. There is no end to this because there is always something new to explore in the endless sea of content that exists via the Internet. In the middle of this, we often lose track of the things that are truly important right in front of us. If we aren't careful, we can neglect our family, goals, relationships and key areas in a way that radically diminishes our quality of life. All because we have given away our precious ability to be present in our lives.

The Need it Now Syndrome. If there is one thing that technology has taught us, it is that we need things right away, like now. Because everything is immediate on social media, our brain has been programmed to expect gratification to come instantly.

This can have dire consequences when it comes to pursuing our most important things in life. Why? Because the coolest things in life flat out take discipline, grit and hard work over extended periods of time. If you expect instant, you will get frustrated quickly and quit before you even have a chance to close the gap on your goals. In simple terms, if you value and expect instant, then you will find yourself making in-the-moment decisions that hurt your family, faith, finances, goals, health and relationships.

Crushing Our Creative Flow. We often don't realize it, but technology has taken up valuable real estate in our brains. This extends far beyond just robbing us of our ability to be present in our most important life areas. The constant urge to pick up our phones has now invaded the creative part of our brains and started to make some of our mannerisms more robotic in nature. With each new technology-driven dopamine hit, we have less and less space to utilize the creative part of our brains. It is slowly draining us of one of the coolest gifts that make us human: the ability to assess our lives and consider a future that we are passionate about pursuing. We are becoming so consumed with immediate that we are giving away our ability to dream up visions that drive our daily behaviors and make the world a cooler place. If you are currently struggling with the vision blueprint process, this may just be the reason why.

THE REAL LIFE IMPLICATIONS
OF INSTANT GRATIFICATION

It makes total sense when you read about the implications of technology and the instant gratification mindset. Honestly, these impacts were never hard for me to wrap my brain around. Intuitively, I completely understood that technology can prime your brain to expect easy and instant. I also knew that hopping on your phone non-stop can rob you of the ability to be present in the most important areas of your life.

Yet for some reason, it was difficult for me to tangibly connect it to my life in a way that grabbed my attention and demanded change. It seems like this is often the case with harmful habits in our society. I needed to get crystal clear on the actual impact of my current mindset so I could avoid this pitfall. I knew this was the only way that I was going to get the leverage to change my patterns.

As I was writing this chapter, I started paying closer attention to my habits. I wanted to see just how much technology was robbing me of the precious present. It didn't take me long to realize that I was allowing instant to consistently dictate the pace in my most important value areas. I noticed there were immediate incongruencies in my stated values and actual real life behaviors. I was saying that family was my top value, but when push came to shove, I was constantly picking up my phone in the evenings when I should have been spending quality time with them. I realized that I was being completely inauthentic in my approach.

This wasn't the only consequence of my instant technology habit. It also flooded my brain and unknowingly tricked me into adopting the "Need It Now Syndrome." This became crystal clear to me one afternoon when I was sitting in my office doing speaking outreach to associations across the United States.

As I finished sending out my 10th email for what was now my 21st consecutive day, I felt myself becoming frustrated that I was not getting the results I desired. *Why am I not landing more talks? My schedule should be full now.*

I was dwelling on these thoughts when I stumbled upon a video of a successful, established speaker who explained that their norm was to send out at least 100 emails every single day. *100!* This blew my mind and instantly became an eye opener because it made me realize that I was not doing near enough to earn the outcomes I desired. I was so consumed with needing it now that I had never actually done the research necessary to determine the process required to close the gap on my goals.

It didn't take me long to realize that this same pattern was carrying over into my relationships. I got frustrated far too easily when my kids didn't act the way I thought they should right away. The same thing would happen if I didn't immediately get the things I wanted from my wife. Listen, there is nothing wrong with desiring certain outcomes in key relationships in your life. The problem is that I believed I deserved them instantly when I had not done near enough to earn them. I had not intentionally poured into my kids to the point that they understood the lessons that were important to me. I also had not done near enough for my wife to expect the outcomes I desired from her.

The final observation I had came in the area of crushing my creative flow. It was a gorgeous Tuesday afternoon in the San Juan Islands so my wife and I decided to head to our favorite spot, Rosario Beach, to do a little work. This was my outdoor location of choice to write because it is absolutely stunning and almost always immediately puts me in a calm, inspired state. I was feeling totally relaxed and in a groove when I felt my phone that was sitting right next to me vibrate. I didn't think anything of it as I picked it up to check my email. Naturally, I strolled over to Facebook to check my updates after this before heading back to writing. Guess what happened less than five minutes later? Yep, I repeated the process. Then I proceeded to do this at lea*st six more times in the next hour.*

I honestly never thought anything of this until I was listening to a podcast one day on maximizing productivity. It was outlining how technology has become one of the biggest drainers on our ability to produce because it interrupts our work flow. I immediately realized that this was *exactly* what was happening to me on a consistent basis while working. Every time I picked up my phone during my work sessions, I was literally draining my creative ENERGY and putting myself back into a beginning phase. I had no shot of getting into a zone that would bring out my best work until I learned to put my phone away. It was time to put it in another room in airplane mode so I could get back to creating something special in the key areas of my life.

ONE SIMPLE QUESTION

I was in the middle of writing this instant chapter when I subtly arrived at a break though insight. I was reading *Change Your Brain, Change Your Life* in my morning routine when the author Dr. Daniel Amen posed a simple question:

Is your behavior getting you what you want?

My first initial reaction was, *What behavior?*

I instantly followed this up with, *getting me what exactly*?

For this second part of the question, I realized almost immediately that I had the answer because I had been pointing my brain to this exact thing for over two months with my value visions. It was this activity that had programmed my brain to know exactly what I wanted in my most important life areas.

I knew that I wanted to create a dynamic environment at home where everyone felt loved unconditionally and were able to completely be themselves. I wanted to find time every single day to pour into them so I could make moments that they would always remember.

In my role as coach (career), I was passionate about writing a book that would help millions of readers break down barriers and pull out their highest potential.

In the area of vitality, I wanted to make lifestyle decisions daily that would maximize ENERGY and allow me to be a charger for the most important people in my life.

I had invested in my value system and knew exactly what I wanted.

Once I reminded myself of exactly what I wanted in my life, Dr. Amen's question actually became pretty simple to answer.

This gave me a solid starting point, but now I needed to tweak the question to make it my own so it would put me into an inspired state. I was immediately drawn to one of my top value drivers, EARN It. This was a key focal point I had been using to drive my intentional behavior on a consistent daily basis. It made sense to incorporate it into the process. After a little reflection, I came up with a new, powerful question that gave me immediate clarity and focus:

Am I EARNING extraordinary in the areas of life (values) that I am most passionate about?

This one single question became the primer that drove me to start flipping the script on easy and instant gratification in my life.

THE FLIP FROM EASY TO EARN IT

The answer to my new question was an unequivocal "no" at the moment. I was not doing near enough to EARN extraordinary in any of my top value areas. I wasn't willing to settle for status quo so I searched for a redirect that would empower my potential. It took me a little reflection, but I eventually found a new question that guided my brain to better options: *What shifts can I make in my behavior to flip the script on easy/instant and EARN extraordinary?* This question was so important because it didn't keep me stuck in a place where I found myself dwelling on disappointment. Instead, it gave me some immediate focal points that would allow me to get out and close the gap on the outcomes that I desired.

Answering this second question led me to a variety of simple strategies that radically elevated my efficiency and effectiveness in my top value areas. One of the most important shifts I committed to making was giving my family, career, vitality, growth and faith a prominent space in my life. If they were going to approach extraordinary, every single one of these value areas deserved my most precious time, ENERGY and focus on a consistent daily basis. It was never going to be enough to simply say they were my top values. I needed to show it by giving them allocated space on my calendar.

It didn't take me long to realize that it was not going to be enough to just schedule time for these values. The coolest accomplishments are never handed to us for simply showing up. Instead, I knew I needed to lock in and find creative ways to bring the best I had to offer to these new "Sacred Space" time frames. It turns out I still had one nasty habit robbing me of doing this in my top value areas. *Can you guess the culprit?* It was my cell phone and Internet access on my laptop. While I had scheduled time to focus on my key roles, I kept hopping on my devices during these time frames which interrupted my creative flow and ability to embrace the precious present. It was time for a more radical approach. This is when I decided to extend my "no technology time" (NTT) philosophy to additional pockets throughout my day.

When your values truly matter, it is your obligation to give them the absolute best you have to offer so they have a chance to become extraordinary. Interestingly, technology was not even close to breaking into my top five values and never would be. Yet here it was getting my most precious ENERGY and was dictating the pace in my life more than anything else. Under no circumstances could I justify it being remotely close to my top values in terms of importance. It was time to flip the script on technology so I could be authentic to my top values. How? By carving out key "Sacred Space" time frames in my day where technology would disappear. These NTT shifts became catalysts for incredible change in my life.

What did this actually look like in my day-to-day life? Well, it all kicked off when I established a rule that I would not touch my phone during the first hour of my day while moving through my morning growth routine. I knew this was one of my single most important "Sacred Space" time periods because it would set the tone for everything else in my life. It would serve as a catalyst to flip the script on instant because it would train my brain to put first things first. On top of this, it would set the tone for my new lifestyle by maximizing the importance of my top values while minimizing the importance of technology. This ended up being a shift with compounding benefits.

I followed this initial step up by identifying a couple of other NTT "Sacred Space" time periods during my day. I intentionally allocated precious time, ENERGY and focus to both my career and family areas. Once I blocked out time for writing this book, I would leave my phone upstairs, turn my Internet off and give each chapter my full attention. I made it an absolute top priority to eliminate all distractions so I could maximize my creative flow during writing time. In the evenings, I left my phone in my bedroom on silent mode so I could be more present during our new 60-minute NTT family fun time. Interestingly, once the phone was gone, it was far easier to lock in and have a blast making moments with my crew.

The final step that I implemented was to use the EARN It mantra in my daily routine to reinforce the shift. When I went through my morning routine, I reminded myself to EARN extraordinary in my value vision areas. Whenever I transitioned into a "Sacred Space" time frame, I urged myself to step up and EARN the outcomes I desired in my life. I did the same thing each time I recognized myself falling into old patterns of expecting easy. Eventually the repetitions from all of these steps morphed together to form an entirely new mindset where I despised the idea of easy and instant. In their place, I started to see myself as a person who was crazy unique because I was showing up and EARNING extraordinary.

EASY NOW = HARDER LATER

I was sitting in my kitchen brainstorming with my wife Brandy about this chapter when I had a startling realization.

If you choose easy now, you will ALWAYS get harder later.

It was the type of thought that immediately grabbed ahold of me and caught my full attention. I knew I had something special when Brandy immediately picked up her notebook to write it down. She replied to me, "Ooooh, that's good. I'm going to steal your knowledge." So, if you catch her posting about this on social media, you totally know who gets credit for it. I'm totally kidding. I am not worried about credit one bit. What is far more important to me is that you grasp the transformational nature of the concept. It will ensure that you make daily decisions that shape a much more inspiring future.

While mulling over this concept, the first thing that immediately popped into my mind was parenting. Why? Because easy has become so simple to choose in this role. If your kids start acting like wild animals, all we have to do is give them an iPad and it will immediately alleviate the situation. How do I know this? My wife and I have both used these "magical" devices to keep our kids at bay while we were working. Heck, I might as well be honest with you. We have used them on more than one occasion to get a little peace and quiet at the end of a busy day. This is one of the quickest and easiest ways to not have to deal with their boredom, bickering and backtalk. It seems totally harmless in the moment, but this process made me realize that there is a weighty decision being made here that deserves our attention.

Every time my wife and I choose easier with electronic devices, it makes life simple now. Our kids get lost in their iPad entertainment and we get to do pretty much whatever we want. But make no mistake about it, there are always consequences to our decisions. In these instances, we were unknowingly deciding to allow a technological device to parent our kids. The thing that eventually caught my attention was the fact that we were unknowingly teaching them to choose instant. On top of this, we were robbing them of opportunities to build meaningful relationships with us. I immediately reminded myself that it was easier now, but there would be nothing easy about this decision later.

I don't know about you, but there are some prices that I am not willing to pay. Once my wife and I became clear about what was at stake, it was an easy decision to make. We both flat out despised the idea of choosing easy with our kids because it meant MUCH harder later in the form of shallow relationships with two of the most important people in our lives. Neither one of us wanted anything to do with our kids not knowing how much we loved them because we were too busy choosing our mobile devices and the easiest path. We also weren't willing to give up opportunities to teach them lessons that would make their lives special down the road. So we decided to stop choosing easy and instead chose options that were more challenging in the moment. This was such a HUGE decision in our life.

This concept doesn't just apply to parenting. I think you already know that. It applies to pretty much every single area of our life that is important to us. In some ways, areas like finances and health are far easier to grasp because they have more immediate tangible outcomes. If you get in the habit of choosing easy with your health behaviors, then you are far more likely to attract outcomes that bring you unbearable pain down the road. In simple terms, pizza and desserts daily can be fun now, but it will wreak havoc on your life in the future in the form of drained ENERGY, increased weight gain and greater chances of severe health risks.

Here's the thing to remind yourself.

The hard you get later will always be so much more challenging than the hard you have to face now with self-discipline.

The same is true with finances, relationships and any other meaningful goal you are pursuing. When you get in the habit of allowing technology to program your brain to expect instant, you are leading yourself down a path to disappointment and pain.

WILL YOU <u>EARN</u> EXTRAORDINARY...OR SETTLE FOR FLIPPIN ORDINARY?

There is one final step that was absolutely essential to me flipping the script on instant gratification. In the middle of this process, I knew the consequences of my current mindset and was flat out not willing to pay the cost of them down the road. The single biggest shift in this area came when I finally answered this question:

Will you EARN extraordinary?

The answer was a definite "yes" for me.

I was personally no longer willing to allow myself to choose instant and easy in the most important areas of my life. Instead, I was going to do everything in my power to EARN the outcomes I desired. I determined that I would choose inconvenient every single day of the week if that is what it took to get extraordinary down the road. My family, career, vitality, growth and faith were unequivocally worth that. I made a resolution to myself that I would never fall into the trap of settling for the status quo in these areas.

When you make the decision to EARN extraordinary in your top value vision areas, it doesn't mean that life all of a sudden gets easier. It just means you have made it a must to fight for the things that matter to you most.

I honestly had to practice what I am preaching while writing this book. As I worked on this chapter, I constantly asked myself if I was willing to show up and EARN uncommon. When you are getting up at 4:30am pushing for a breakthrough on a chapter, it can be challenging to come by. But each time I asked if I was willing to EARN extraordinary, my answer was always "yes" so I kept pushing for it. It was through this decision to EARN IT that I finally started to find the direction for this book and my voice as an author. It never would have happened if I didn't flip the script on instant and commit to doing what was necessary to write a book that would pour into people's lives.

This is the one question you need to answer yourself right now if you want to flip the script on instant gratification:

Am I willing to EARN extraordinary?

It's necessary to make this decision ahead of time because you are going to need it in your journey. Why? Well, in my experience, I have learned that life is always going to send you challenges to test whether or not you are serious about the outcomes you desire. When those times come, it's so important that you have already pre-determined how you will deal with them. If you have made EARNING it an absolute must, you will continue to show up no matter what life sends your way. Once you have made this resolute decision, you are different and it's a matter of time until you create results that make your life remarkable and memorable.

This reminds me of a quote that came out of an Earn the Right podcast interview I did with 21x NCAA Champion coach Anson Dorrance.

If you don't get up every single morning committed to closing the gap on your goals, there's nothing wrong with you. You're just ordinary and you need to get used to being ordinary.

I want to ask you a quick, defining question right now.

Are you cool with settling for flippin ordinary in the most important areas of your life?

If you are, then you might want to put this book down and search for another one that allows you to settle for average. Since you are still reading, I don't get the sense that you want this at all.

Now that we have settled that. Let's move forward eager to embrace the challenges that inevitably come when you pursue your highest potential.

FLIPPIN INSTANT

One of my goals in each chapter is to make you sick and tired of the negative patterns we are covering. Why? Because these are likely the exact habits that are robbing you of the ability to create the results and life you desire. This chapter gets my blood boiling because technology and instant gratification is stopping so many people from closing the gap on their goals and pulling out their highest potential. It also happens to be leading them straight to d-emotions (disappointing emotions) that create a drag on their lives.

Here's the thing. It doesn't have to be this way and I think you now realize that. I believe deep inside my core that you are capable of extraordinary in your life. I just hope that I have done enough to spark a fire inside you that is passionate about flipping the script on instant so you can EARN extraordinary in the key areas of your life moving forward.

THE SACRED SPACE "EARN IT" HABIT

This fourth yellow ball activity is designed to help you flip the script on instant gratification so you can close the gap on the results you desire in life. The cool thing is that this activity is specifically designed to build on our previous Value Vision habit. However, this one is going to be a little different because it is going to involve some initial reflection so you can identify areas where instant gratification is halting your progress. Once you have identified these areas, our job is to train your brain to embrace an uncommon approach that allows you to EARN extraordinary moving forward. You can follow the three steps below to make this happen.

1. Ask the Instant Reflection Question: *Am I EARNING extraordinary in each of the areas of my life (values) that I am most passionate about?* If the answer is "yes" here, move to #3 and find new ways to elevate your efforts.

2. Ask the Instant Redirect Question: *If not, what shifts can I make in my behavior to flip the script on easy/instant and EARN extraordinary?*

3. Intentionally schedule NTT "Sacred Space" time frames each day for your top 2-3 value areas. Even if technology is not an issue, focus on blocking out distractions so you can give your top priorities the best you have to offer. As you transition into each planned time slot, remind yourself to "EARN It" so you maximize your chances to achieving extraordinary in your top value areas.

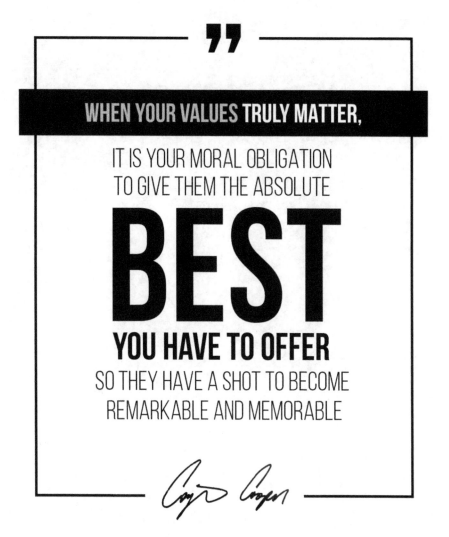

"

WHEN YOUR VALUES TRULY MATTER,

IT IS YOUR MORAL OBLIGATION
TO GIVE THEM THE ABSOLUTE

BEST

YOU HAVE TO OFFER

SO THEY HAVE A SHOT TO BECOME
REMARKABLE AND MEMORABLE

FLIP ING FLAWLESS

NOT PERFECT...JUST PASSION

"No matter how small you start, start something that matters."
—Brendon Burchard

As I walked up on stage, I was definitely way more nervous than normal. My hands were a smidge fidgety and my knees felt a little like Jell-O. I silently told myself that this was to be expected when you are giving your first TEDx Talk. The whole concept of full pre-rehearsals with other speakers critiquing performance was foreign to me as well so I reminded myself not to make a big deal about my unexpected nerves. Just like when I was competing in big tournaments as an elite athlete, these jitters started to subside as I moved through my talk. I made it through my speech in the right 14-minute time frame, but my delivery was not near as strong as I would have liked it to be. I officially had less than 24-hours to shore it up. I walked off stage looking for a solution so I could calm myself and give myself a shot to deliver a memorable performance.

As I arrived back at my hotel room, I sat and reflected on the practice session. I wondered what had changed in my approach to make me so nervous. I had literally done this hundreds and hundreds of times so it was not normal for me to feel like this while on stage. I felt like I was back at Indiana University that first semester I stepped into the classroom to teach. I knew the question I needed to ask myself. *What was I focused on that was causing me to be nervous?* I knew that emotions were a result of my thinking so I tried to figure out the trigger for these nerves. Once I started to relax, the reason behind my jitters became crystal clear. I had built the talk into something that it wasn't.

For at least five years, I had heard about TEDx Talks and how they were a really big deal. They were the type of talk that could completely change your career and life if you got them just right. I had bought into this belief from the moment I applied and got accepted to do the TEDxHilliard talk. While this might be a true belief, it was the wrong way to be approaching any talk or performance. I had made it into such a big deal that being nervous was inevitable. It certainly wasn't intentional, but I had convinced myself that this talk was a key to breakthrough for my career and family. That is an awful lot of expectation for a 14-minute talk.

Once I realized the problem with my approach, I tried to get back to the basics. I reminded myself that a talk is just a talk. I had learned this from one of the best coaches I ever had as an athlete. It was my high school club coach Ron and he taught me to control my process. Everything was about approaching competition in a consistent manner and to see it as an incredible opportunity. The platform and audience size didn't really matter. What mattered was that I approached this opportunity with the best that I had to offer. Nothing more, nothing less. When you get this right, you are simply walking up on stage and sharing a message that you are passionate about.

The truth is that there was another culprit here that I needed to address before I stepped on stage to give the talk. In hindsight, I realize that this was actually a bigger influence on my nerves than anything else. It also happens to be one of the biggest barriers I face even today as I strive to create experiences that impact millions of lives. I was focused on an ideal outcome that was out of my control. I wanted the talk to be flawless so it would go viral and spread around the world at a rapid pace. I was so focused on this outcome that it was causing me to believe that I needed everything to go perfect to make it happen. Above all, the thing I realized is that I was worrying too much about what the talk would mean for me.

If there is one thing I learned during this experience, it is that nerves are pretty common when you make things too much about yourself. It is the quickest and surest way to make sure that you have negative emotions that start to limit your potential. The good news is that the shift here was simpler than you might think. I reminded myself that I didn't need to be worried about being perfect. This talk was no different than the hundreds I had given before. I just needed to take the focus off of me and make it more about my audience. This is when it hit me that there were two things I always focused on when giving my best performances.

The first was giving. When I threw my ego to the side and reminded myself of the opportunity I had to impact lives, I always gave better talks. Focusing on my audience rather than myself always lowered my nerves because I wasn't focused on what the talk meant for me. I was just locked in on how I could deliver a message that would empower them to potential. I certainly wasn't perfect at doing this all the time, but I had made it a point of emphasis in my approach and it immediately made me a better speaker for obvious reasons. The focus on giving significantly lowered my anxiety levels and allowed me to start approaching my talks with more authenticity and vulnerability.

The second thing I had done was to intentionally focus on growing. I stopped worrying so much about a perfect outcome and instead just reminded myself to embrace getting better every single talk that I gave. I have to admit that this initially had a selfish slant because I had interviewed incredible performers and they all seemed to value and emphasize growth. I figured there must be something to this so I encouraged myself to love the opportunity to grow and morph into a world-class speaker. However, the more I emphasized growth and loving the process, I realized that it was the key to making my anxiety disappear because it allowed me to focus on an outcome that I could always control. It was a game changer for me as a performer.

As I sat in my hotel room reflecting on my TEDx Talk the next day, I realized that I knew the key to creating a shift in my mindset. It was plain as day right in front of me now.

Give and Grow.

That's the mantra I needed to embrace to give myself a shot to perform to potential in my talk. So, I did what made sense; I reminded myself over and over to *Give and Grow* with emotion. Every time I felt some nervousness, I reminded myself that it wasn't my job to be perfect. I just needed to control what I could control. My only job was to show up and give to the audience while emphasizing getting better. Just like that, my anxiety disappeared and I was able to go into my talk ready to perform to potential.

WHAT DOES THIS HAVE TO DO WITH REAL LIFE?

I know what you might be thinking to yourself right now. *Great Coyte! I am happy for you, but what does this have to do with me and my life? I am not a speaker and I don't have any interest in improving my performance on stage. Heck, I would rather avoid being in front of anyone giving a talk!* Ok, I admit that I might have exaggerated that response a smidge, but I do believe that some of you will be questioning the application to normal everyday living. I hear you completely, but stay with me here because there is an incredible opportunity for change in the middle of this philosophy. It might not seem like it on the surface, but the emphasis on giving and growing can radically elevate every area of your life that truly matters to you. Let me give you some examples from my past coaching clients. I believe you will eventually connect the dots once you see the similarities here.

- A mother of two who needed things to go perfectly in their household to feel like they were enough as a parent.

- A sales professional who needed to close every single sale to feel like they were successful in their job.

- An athlete who needed every competition to go just as planned to be able to feel like they were excelling in their sport.

- A real estate professional who needed every single interaction to be positive for them to proceed with prospecting in their job.

- A starting speaker who needed to get 150 likes and 50 shares on every single post to feel like they were reaching people.

- A thought leader who wanted everyone to agree with their ideas to believe that they are great at their calling.

All of these people had one thing in common: *they had expectations that were unreasonable.* Because of this, these well-intentioned people were destined to fail because the outcomes they desired were unattainable. Making matters worse, they had set themselves up to experience disappointment on the backend because they had associated pain with falling short of expectations. Anything less than perfect would lead right to disappointment. How likely is it that their brain will willingly move towards the outcomes they desire if they expect to experience pain? Not likely at all. When we stack the deck against ourselves by expecting perfection, we are almost guaranteed to settle in our lives.

Before we talk about the shifts here, I have to confess something. I lied to you just a little bit on the list I just gave you. Not because the examples aren't true. Every single one of them are real life examples of mindsets pulling down people's potential.

What I did not tell you in the moment was that the last two examples were me.

I am not necessarily thrilled to admit that, but I think it is important for me to be honest if we are going to get anywhere special with this book. I owe you the truth.

The social media one is a little embarrassing to admit, but it is also a really good example of the subtle perfection plague that can invade our lives if we aren't aware of our beliefs. I realize now that I had an idea in my head of how many people needed to respond to my posts to consider them a success. Do you know what I did when they didn't meet this expectation? I deleted them. Most of the time I didn't even give them a chance to play out over the course of a day.

I now realize that my expectations were wrong for a number of reasons.

What if that post would have reached one person and encouraged them to boldly pursue their dreams?

What if leaving the post up would have helped a struggling mom find the positive in their day?

Heck, what if leaving the post up would have led to a powerful breakthrough in my life?

The one thing I know for certain is that taking them down wasn't allowing me to learn the process necessary to reach more people.

I'm not alone here. I have worked with enough clients and people to know that this is far more common than you might think. I already gave you several examples in this section alone that are pretty routine in our society. In every single instance, perfection was robbing these people of their ability to go out and create meaningful outcomes in their life. In the process, it was also subtly stealing their happiness and ability to create vibrant emotions that made their life dynamic. The awesome news is that I had learned how to break through this perfection plague. I just needed to teach them to flip the script on flawless by focusing on giving and growing in their most important roles.

NOT COMPLETELY CURED

I wish I could tell you that the one successful *Give and Grow* shift during my TEDx Talk cured me of my perfection plague. It definitely helped me excel in my speaking career because it allowed me to start delivering with more authenticity and vulnerability. But it didn't naturally carry over into the other applicable areas of my life. Isn't it fascinating how this works? You can implement a powerful concept into one important area of your life that makes a profound difference, but it isn't a universal application. It's also intriguing that we don't immediately make the connection to other areas and intentionally apply it to maximize the rewards that we reap. I know I certainly hadn't done this.

Think about it a little bit. I would be willing to bet that you have an area of your life where you are thriving. It is almost guaranteed that this has come to fruition because of your focus and ability to take intentional action. You have stumbled upon a winning strategy. Yet there is a good chance that you haven't taken these impactful lessons and intentionally applied them to other key areas of your life. I bet it had not even crossed your mind to do so. If so…*Phew, I am not alone!*

I didn't realize the connection here until I was in the middle of a mini-slump in my work. I was showing up to EARN my aspirations, but there was something holding me up. Have you ever felt this way? You are scheduling time to invest in your goals and vision, but you don't seem to be making meaningful progress. This was totally me early in this journey. I had all these visions that I was excited about pursuing, but I kept hesitating when it came time to go all in to get the outcomes I desired. I really wanted to, but there was something tugging at me that was stopping me from cutting loose.

This is when I realized that my issue was that I wanted everything to go perfect right out of the gates.

I have to admit that this was one of my biggest barriers when writing large chunks of this book. Ironically, it was certainly the case when starting to build out a structure for this chapter. I wanted to be able to have the content flow seamlessly straight from my brain to the computer screen on the first draft. *I wanted a profound, life altering chapter in one clean writing session.* This came from a good authentic place, but my approach was entirely wrong. It wasn't a reasonable expectation at all and it sounds ridiculous reflecting and writing about it now. Once I realized that my belief system was irrational, I turned my attention to a shift so I could flip the script on perfection once and for all.

Fortunately, I kept stepping until I found a solution. I connected some dots and came to realize that the only way to navigate this obstacle was to embrace being a beginner. I had to learn to write with no plans for perfection. This was challenging for me at first because I had a counterproductive engrained belief in my head of what it took to be exceptional at something. It took breaking down this "flawless" focal point to make real progress in my career. I started to remind myself that it wasn't my job to be perfect. My job was to clear the clutter and deliver messages I was crazy passionate about sharing with the world. It didn't matter if my writing was kind of rotten at first. I had to be willing to start so I could get the right ideas in place.

A fascinating shift started to occur after I started to shun the idea of perfection. I started to breakthrough in my writing. Ideas started to flow onto the screen and I was able to start to piecing them together in a logical manner. It was in the middle of this process that I had a mind blowing insight that stopped me in my tracks.

My best writing comes when I see myself as a beginner.

Don't misunderstand me here. I am not saying that I believed I was a writer with no clue how to put a book together. Instead, I simply saw myself as a person who was starting a new journey and needed to figure out how to navigate my path. Each page was something fresh I had never done before and I needed to embrace that. I had to learn to love navigating new voyages where I had no initial idea where I was going.

It turns out that this is exactly what I needed to do in all areas of my life. I needed to completely purge the idea of perfection and instead focus on pursuing passion. This allowed me to stop hesitating on the courses and live events I was creating. This is when another startling realization hit me.

I was totally capable of creating world-class experiences that would transform people's lives, but only if I was first willing to be average at it to start. I could have all of my wildest dreams if I was just able to let my guard down and embrace being a beginner. I needed to break down any remaining expectations of perfection and instead learn to love my process.

I have come to believe that this is one of the single biggest barriers that proactive people face in their lives. They want to create remarkable outcomes that truly matter, but they aren't willing to embrace the early part of the journey. There is a perception in our society that strength comes from the ability to always excel at things immediately and it simply isn't true. Every extraordinary person on the planet has had a point in their lives when they just had to be willing to start. It required them to step into uncertainty and accept that they would not be great at their new endeavor at the start. They accepted this, but then started showing up daily passionate to hone their craft. Eventually this allowed them to excel as they became one of the few willing to stick it out long enough to EARN extraordinary. It turns out that this is exactly what we need to do to flip the script on flawless.

THE REAL UNDERLYING CAUSE

Do you know what I learned about myself during this process? Sometimes the pursuit of perfection is not exactly what it appears to be. On the surface, it seemed like I was striving for flawless because it was the ideal standard for excellence. *It's what you do when you are a person who is passionate about achieving at a high level.* But what I also started to realize was that there was something working under the surface that didn't support this notion. For me, it was the fact that perfection was a mask. One that was covering up my fear of failure and not being enough. We are going to address these more in-depth in a later chapter, but I needed to point them out here as a reference point.

With some reflection, I started to recognize that my idea of perfection was actually an excuse. By focusing on perfection, I had given myself an end outcome that was impossible to achieve. At the end of the day, this allowed me to always have a reason to draw back on my dreams. The truth is that I was scared to go all in to get my goals. I had failed at UNC and my brain wanted to keep me safe in this new endeavor. So it grabbed onto perfection and used it as a crutch. Whenever I didn't take action to close the gap on my desired outcomes, I could simply chalk it up to the fact that I was a perfectionist. I needed more time to prepare so I could make it flawless before releasing it to people. Perfection became a way for me to hold back and play it safe in the comfort of my own home.

Yet we both know that this type of approach isn't productive at all. Holding back on pursuing your dreams does not keep you safe. Sure it allows you to avoid the pain that sometimes comes when you are rejected pursuing things you love, but it also puts you directly on a path that will guarantee one of the greatest pains of all. The one where you give up on your dreams and settle for less than you are capable of in your life. I started to realize that this was one of my biggest barriers. My perception of perfection was holding me up from going out and freeing up my highest potential. It was time to flip it so I could have a fresh perspective that would inject more passion into my life.

THE FLIP FROM PERFECTION TO PASSION

My next flip came when I realized that the *Give and Grow* concept was the key in this situation to freeing up my potential. I didn't need to be perfect to do either one of these things. Instead, I just needed to train my brain to make them a primary focal point so I could redirect to productive during my days. It made sense to add this to my morning growth routine as an area of emphasis as I went through each of my value visions. I now realize that this was the start of a new yellow ball habit that made my perfection plague disappear. Well, at least it started to chip away and become far less prevalent.

These redirects became a part of a combined process to flip the script on flawless. By focusing on giving, it tapped into a part of me that was waiting to get out. I had been so concerned about myself throughout my tenure decision that I had forgotten to think about others. In a state of scarcity, it hadn't occurred to me that I should be more concerned with serving the people around me. This simple shift became a catalyst to change that. As I started to focus on giving more to the people around me, I ended up getting one of the coolest gifts you can receive in life: *passion.* At first it was a small spark, but the more I gave, the more my passion morphed into a fire that started to drive every aspect of my life.

The same exact thing happened with growth. Each day that I invested in getting better, it started to pull more gifts out of me. In the process, I started to find myself. It was as if I was finally learning who I was put on this planet to be. In the middle of this transformation, I became even more passionate about my new approach because I knew it was the catalyst for pulling out purpose and passion in my life. This is when I started to realize the significance of the shift I had just made. All along, I had been honing my ability to flip the script on flawless and the idea of perfection. This flip eventually manifested from one additional mindset shift that acted as an anchor for this powerful redirect.

Not perfect…just passion.

This was the focal point I harnessed to finally flip the script on my perfection plague. I trained my brain to believe that I never had to be perfect. It wasn't my job to be flawless. That mindset and approach would only bring me anxiety because it was unattainable. It would drive me into a frustrating loop where I consistently drew back on the pursuit of my dreams. My only job now was to pursue passion. That's it. I just needed to get up each day and pursue the things I loved all out. I knew without a shadow of a doubt that I was capable of making this happen. It inspired me to realize that I was capable of owning my destiny if I pursued focal points (*Give and Grow*) that were always in my control.

I can't explain why, but I suddenly knew that my efforts would always be enough if I just followed this simple formula. I wasn't being naïve. I understood that there would be times when I fell short of expectations. It was just no longer an issue because I now had a solution for when it occurred. I would simply redirect my brain to giving and growing so I could control my process. If I did this often enough, I had a feeling that it would eventually lead me to an extraordinary place in my life. It might not be the exact place I had in mind, but it would be somewhere worthy of my highest potential.

These "small" shifts completely freed me up. I was no longer being drug down by the perception that I needed to be perfect. Every time I sat down to work, I reminded myself to embrace the journey.

Be a beginner Coyte!

Love getting out and EARNING the right to close the gap on your goals!

Just pursue passion today and the outcomes will take care of themselves!

It was this programming that allowed me to start releasing my creativity and potential into my work.

Not perfect…just passion!

Every time I reminded myself of this, it was as if I released a weight that had been dragging behind me. It was the most incredible thing because I started to feel lighter in every part of my life. This allowed me to start pursuing my goals in a far more efficient manner.

PURSUE PASSION AS A PRIORITY

I was writing this chapter one day when a powerful thought hit me. *Passion isn't going to show up at your doorstep every single day to wake you up. You MUST get up each morning and pursue it all out if you want it to have a prominent place in your life.* I realized that I had started to pull out passion in my life by actively giving and growing on a consistent daily basis. But something was telling me that this wasn't quite enough to sustain meaningful motion in my life.

That is when I had another breakthrough insight that guided me down the right path.

Stop worrying so much about everything and just PURSUE PASSION.

I am not certain why, but this message spoke to me in a way that just made sense. I guess you could say that I was ready to hear it because I had been emphasizing the give and grow philosophy in my life. Now I wanted to take things to an entirely different level. The idea of actively pursuing passion fired me up so I decided to make it an emphasis in my daily routine. It wasn't all that complicated really. I just woke up and urged myself to PURSUE PASSION in the key areas of my life. I made the decision to stop waiting around for it and instead started actively pursuing it.

I have to admit that the seed thought for this shift came from inspiration that I received from a good friend of mine, Jim Miller. Jim is a former 10x NCAA Champion coach at the University of Wartburg in the sport of wrestling. He is also one of the most motivating people I have ever met in my life. Jim absolutely oozes enthusiasm, ENERGY and inspiration whenever you are around him. I was interviewing him for a podcast episode one day when I asked him about the topic of motivation. *How do you stay motivated?* He explained that so many people wait around to be motivated so they can achieve their goals. Not Jim. Instead, he explained that he just tells himself to "be motivated." I started to understand why he was one of the most motivating people I had ever met. It wasn't an option for him. He saw it as an obligation to get up and be motivated on a consistent daily basis for himself and the people around him.

When I reflected on Jim's approach, I realized that passion is pretty much the same. That's why I got up and started to own my passion for living. I just decided that I would intentionally pursue it in my days. This might seem like a simple shift on the surface, but the truth is that it fundamentally changed how I approached every important value area in my life. It made me realize that it was no longer enough to just go through the motions. I should have known this, but I had been so busy with the crazy clutter of living that I had missed it. I alone was responsible for the passion in my own life. Nobody else. I knew at this exact moment that if I stepped up and owned this, I would always have the emotion necessary to create real motion and momentum in my life.

While we are here, let me tell you a little about what this looked like in my day-to-day living. Rather than coasting in my parenting duties, I reminded myself to pursue passion and show my kids what it looked like to live all out every single day. Instead of just putting together chapters in this book in a methodical way, I pushed myself to write about things that spoke to my soul and that I was crazy passionate about sharing. I stopped allowing myself to mail it in while posting messages on social media. Instead, I urged myself to remember that I had an opportunity to inspire people with every single interaction I had with them. If I was going to do this right, I owed it to myself and my followers to bring real passion to everything that I did.

PASSION AND THE TWO POSSIBLES

It's about time to wrap this chapter up, but before I do that, I want to bring up a couple of things about passion. If you are going to flip the script on flawless, then this is your area of emphasis. *Not perfect…just passion.* It is always within your power to make this redirect and radically elevate your life. To drive this process home, I want to share a concept with you that I call *Passion and the Two Possibles.* These were game changers for me because they changed the way I saw passion in my day-to-day living. It became an absolute must once I fully realized what was at stake.

The first thing that I realized was that *passion is ALWAYS possible.* This was something that I needed to own with all my mental muscle if I was going to truly flip the script on flawless. I couldn't see it as situational and out of my control. Instead, I needed to see it more like Jim Miller and embrace it as an opportunity. No matter what I was facing in life, I could choose a perspective point that would pull out passion and inspire me to find an entirely different level. To illustrate this point, let's take a situation that I faced during my journey that I outlined in my TEDx Talk: changing my daughter Mya's nasty blowout diaper.

I was writing one morning when my daughter came up and said, "Daddy, I have poopy on my finger." I was sure it was chocolate milk, but as she turned around, I realized that her assessment was spot on because she had poop running all the way up her back and in between her shoulder blades. As I followed her over to the changing table, I despised the idea of changing this diaper. I was focused on all the wrong things when I stopped and reminded myself of the power of choice. It was at this moment that I reminded myself that there were parents all over the world that had lost their children and would trade me in a second for this opportunity. *Perspective.* In an instant, I felt blessed for the opportunity and felt a deep passion for being able to love my daughter.

I started to apply this philosophy to every area of my life as often as possible. There were all kids of moments early on writing this book that were really difficult for me because I wasn't quite sure exactly what to do. I was focused on it being an obligation when I reminded myself to shift my perspective point. This wasn't some dirty diaper I was unfortunate to change. It was an opportunity. Nobody was forcing me to write this book. I CHOSE to write it. It was a flippin chance to radically change lives and it was my job to always see it this way! A fascinating thing happened when I started to see the key areas of my life as an opportunity. It started to pull out passion that had been dormant inside of me. *Passion is ALWAYS possible!*

The second thing I started to realize is that *passion makes extraordinary possible.* Think about it. Every incredible accomplishment that the world has ever seen has one thing in common. This is the same for the extraordinary lives that unique people string together. They are always driven by passion. This is the secret sauce for creating a life that is remarkable and memorable. When you take away passion, you simply don't have what it takes to show up every single day and EARN the outcomes that will make your life dynamic and vibrant. It is this desire to have enthusiasm, ENERGY and inspiration in your life that will keep you getting up and fighting to live your dreams.

Here is what I know to be true from working with thousands and thousands of people. All across the United States and the world, people have an urge for their lives to stand for something special. They want to find their purpose and pull out their highest potential, but they don't know exactly how to make this happen. I believe it deep down in my core that you are capable of incredible things in your life. That is, IF you get up each morning and remind your brain to pursue passion all out in the value areas that are most important to you. It is improbable that you will ever make this happen if life feels like an obligation to you. When you start to see it as an opportunity, then passion will begin to ooze out of you.

Why is this so important to me? Because I learned that my brain only pays close attention to my conscious thoughts when real emotion enters the equation. It's a way to make sure that my most important things get the attention they deserve from my subconscious brain. But there is another essential benefit that warrants consideration. Your brain isn't the only thing that will take notice here. God will take notice. The universe will take notice. Whoever it is that you think is in charge will take notice. I truly believe that passion is rewarded because it is a high-level emotion and ENERGY source that makes the world a much better and cooler place.

FLIPPIN FLAWLESS

Perfection is actually a lot like poop. It stinks and lowers the quality of your life if you allow it to stay too long. The moment I realized what a focus on flawless was doing to my life, I immediately decided that it was time for a change. I needed a fresh start that would allow me to pull out my highest potential. This is when I adopted a new focal point that allowed me to flip the script on perfection and avoid the associated stink in the future. Each day that I got up and emphasized giving and growing, it started to pull out a passion that had been lying somewhat dormant inside of me. This became an incredible driver in creating powerful change in my career, life and top value areas.

Here's the truth. Living below your potential is like a dirty diaper. Settling for results in alignment with the status quo will always stink. You don't deserve that in your life. Especially when you are more than capable of swapping it out for a much better option. If you are going to get better in your life, you need to make a decision right now that you will do whatever it takes to change it. Don't allow a limiting perspective you picked to continue to create a drag on your life. Let's shift it out with an empowering focal point that allows you to flip the script on flawless so you can close the gap on your goals and dreams.

YELLOW BALL #5

THE "GIVE AND GROW" HABIT

If we are going to flip the script on flawless, the first step you need to take is being completely honest with yourself about past situations where you have held back on taking action because of a desire to be perfect. It is important that you don't dwell on them during this reflection period. Instead, examine them and consider ways that you could have used the *Give and Grow* philosophy to flip perfection and build momentum. Once you have found shifts that could have served you, it's time to work on applying this concept to the most important areas of your life so you can drum up passion in your approach moving forward. Follow these three steps to flip the script on flawless once and for all.

1. Identify the single most important outcome in your top value area that you are passionate about pursuing in the next 66-days. Notice any hesitation that you might have when thinking about this outcome.

2. Rather than allow perfection or any other mechanism to thwart your efforts, immediately focus on how an emphasis on giving can enhance your efforts. *How can I give more abundantly through my efforts?* Even if this is attracting more abundance to add more value to your family, this is a critical step because it will make it less about you so you can lower your resistance.

3. Once you have finished the previous step, immediately put an emphasis on how the situation can help you grow and maximize your potential. *What types of growth benefits will I receive if I focus on laying it on the line and flat out going for it?* Remind yourself here to make growth an absolute top priority so you can free up completely in your approach.

The key in the second and third steps is to see the outcome in a way that creates excitement in your brain. Leverage the power of perspective here as much as possible. If you train your brain to see the situation as an opportunity, it will be far more likely to pursue it in a positive, high-level emotional state. It will allow you to flip the script on flawless and cultivate a growth mindset that will lead to incredible outcomes in the future.

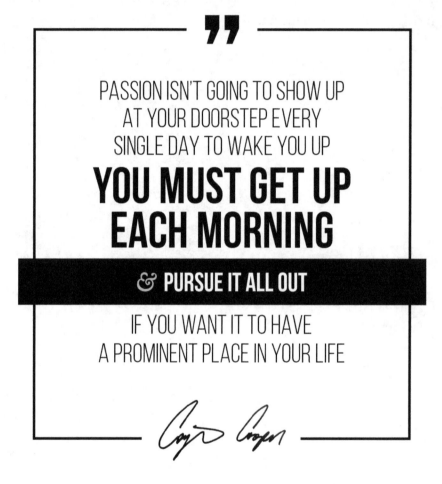

PASSION ISN'T GOING TO SHOW UP
AT YOUR DOORSTEP EVERY
SINGLE DAY TO WAKE YOU UP

YOU MUST GET UP
EACH MORNING

& PURSUE IT ALL OUT

IF YOU WANT IT TO HAVE
A PROMINENT PLACE IN YOUR LIFE

CHAPTER 6

SELF-DOUBT

NOT FIT IN...STAND OUT

"Only misfits and oddballs change the world. It's cool to be a little weird."
—**Robin Sharma**

I was sitting in the office of one of the top ranking administrators at the University of North Carolina. His immaculate space had a massive window featured behind his desk that overlooked the gorgeous quad area. I had scheduled the meeting to ask for clarification on my tenure-decision, but we were more than 15-minutes in and I really didn't have any clarity. At one point, I asked him bluntly, "How is it possible that I could have full support in my department and college and then have a final committee make a completely different decision?" He paused for a few moments to ponder before responding, "Coyte, it's like you are a really good baseball player, but you have been playing cricket and didn't actually know you were playing cricket."

I left this meeting completely deflated. I had hoped that this administrator would consider my pleas and decide to change the decision. In hindsight, I realize that this was never going to happen. The only thing I knew for sure at this moment was that I didn't fit in at the university. At least that is what he had inferred. I had also learned that I was a "really good baseball player" that hadn't realized I had been playing the wrong game for the past six-years of my life. What I think he really meant was that the skill sets that I had brought to the table didn't fit the university. They weren't up to par. It was hard to see it any other way than the top administrators and decision-makers not believing that I was enough to be at the university permanently.

It's a hard pill to swallow when you are rejected by someone or something you truly care about. I definitely wasn't ready for it so it initially turned my life upside down. I found myself wondering what I could have done differently. If I just would have realized I was playing cricket sooner, I could have taken the time to learn the rules and to develop the skill sets to thrive at it. I think I could have been a pretty decent cricket player. But do you know what I eventually realized?

I wasn't a cricket player.

I never was and never would be.

When I actually thought about it, I didn't even have an actual real interest in playing cricket. There's nothing wrong with it at all. It just wasn't the right fit for me and I was glad that I finally recognized that. It was time to move on.

How often do we do this? We try to learn the rules of a game we don't even really have an interest in at all. Then we spend a lot of time trying to hone our skill sets just so we can get permission to be included in the games. In the process, we quit playing the actual sport that we are great at and give up the things we are passionate about. It is a subtle process, but this is exactly when we start to slowly sacrifice the parts of us that actually make us unique. All so we can just fit in and be accepted. Here's the crazy thing. We aren't even convinced that we even flippin like the game we are trying to play!

No, this really has nothing to do with cricket. I'm sure you get that. Maybe the analogy seems like a stretch to you, but I don't believe that it is at all. So often, we stroll through life consistently toning down who we are and strive to adjust our personalities and interests just to be accepted by people we look up to. Heck, this is often done for people who don't even really deserve it. It doesn't really matter who the people are really because that isn't the point. The point is that we literally give up the neatest parts of ourselves just for the chance to be accepted by other people. That isn't right and we both know it.

In hindsight, this is exactly what I had done when I arrived at UNC for what I then considered my dream job. I looked around at my environment and paid attention to all the things my senior faculty members were doing. I made a note of the important rules and did everything I could to make sure I followed them. I wanted to be certain I did everything in my power to fit in so I would be accepted and granted tenure. Obviously, you now know how this ended for me. Now I understand why. I had tried to be something that I wasn't. That was never going to work. Even if I had been granted tenure, I would have ended up being unhappy.

I want to be clear about something.

This was completely my own fault.

Nobody had asked me to adjust who I was. I had scanned my environment upon arrival and made the decision to tone down my personality to fit in. I was to blame for this because it was always within my power to step up and be authentic to my values and what I believed in. I knew one thing for sure:

I was tired of being something I wasn't.

I didn't want to adjust my personality every time I switched my environment.

This was exhausting me and left me feeling inauthentic. I was ready to just be me. ALL THE TIME. I decided that it was my moment to create a set of core attributes that I would strive to live and model no matter who I was around. Rather than trying to fit in, I was ready to step up and embrace an approach outside the status quo.

THE CORE DRIVERS FOR CHANGE

As I went through this reflective process, I knew I no longer wanted to fit in. Every ounce of my being was urging me to step up and go for it in my life. I didn't realize it at the time, but I had already made a decision that was the foundation for flipping the script on my remaining self-doubt. I had decided internally that I would no longer allow myself to fit in no matter what my circumstances were. Instead, I was going to do everything in my power to stand out by living authentically every single day. It was at this point that I knew I needed to figure out precisely what that meant. I wanted to be completely me on a consistent daily basis, but I wasn't exactly sure who that was quite yet.

It sounds weird to admit out loud that I wasn't certain who I was, but it's the honest truth. It's actually far more common than you might think because we are all inundated with messages on exactly what to value from a young age. Add to this the insane clutter that attacks us every single day and you can start to see how easily we get off track. I was ready to stop allowing other people to dictate the pace in my life. I determined that I wanted to shore up exactly who I was passionate about becoming as a human being on a daily basis. This is when I came up with a series of attributes that I now call value drivers that I was committed to living every single day in my life.

I came at identifying these value drivers in a completely unique way. I had done a lot of work on identifying personal values in the past, but that was always from the angle of simply considering the person you were passionate about becoming. This criteria was still going to be in play, but I was going to take a different angle this time around. I decided that I would use one criteria to kickstart this process.

Who did I need to become to EARN the right to live my value visions?

I knew this approach would meet the previous passion criteria because it was driven by value visions I was willing to fight for. However, I had no idea at the time just how much this shift would radically transform my approach to living.

As I mulled over the person I needed to become to live my dreams, I started to stumble upon attributes that sparked something inside of me. It charged me up to think about how I could be more *present* and *giving* to the people that mattered to me most. It gave me a surge of ENERGY to envision myself being more *dynamic* when sharing my message with my audience. It inspired me to realize that being more *curious*, *grateful*, and *energized* would allow me to close the gap on the results I desired in life.

I know I am not the only one who responds to this type of approach. I have seen this same response from the thousands of people I have had the pleasure of working with the past few years in a performance and potential capacity. There is something remarkable that happens when people start to think about the human being they are passionate about becoming en route to their dream life. It taps into a deep reservoir of inspiration because it is the first step to becoming the person you are meant to be.

This happens to be one of the greatest untapped secrets to flipping the script on your highest potential. If you can show your brain a better option that involves purpose, it will always peak its interest. Even if the world around you is chaotic, purpose is the trump card that will always cut through it all and demand your brain to pay attention. When you have this type of redirect, you have the master skill set to flip the script because it will promptly point your brain from problems to possible. The best way to flip the script on self-doubt is to keep pointing your brain to attributes that inspire you to be your absolute best.

Once I had an initial set of value drivers in place that I believed in, I started the programming process. This is a fancy way of saying that I showed up every single day and revisited them during my morning routine.

I went through my values individually and reminded myself to pursue them with a passion.

I urged myself to be more *energized* so I had the opportunity to inspire more people to live to their highest potential.

I passionately encouraged myself to be *curious* and *grateful* in everything that I did so I could maximize my growth and close the gap on the results I desired.

I think you get the point here. I showed up and started to fight for the person I was passionate about becoming. I was officially starting to create an approach that led me to standing out.

ONLY MISFITS AND ODDBALLS CHANGE THE WORLD

Do you know what REALLY helped spark change in this part of my journey? When I started to connect the fact that the coolest people on the planet flat out don't fit in. Think about it. There is nothing normal about the way that people like Bill Gates, Ellen DeGeneres, Oprah Winfrey, Richard Branson, Tony Robbins and Will Smith carry themselves. The reason we watch and admire them is because of their outrageously unique approach to living. In a world where settling for the status quo has become the standard, they have instead chosen to rise up and be their authentic selves. In this way they have made the bold decision to stand out rather than to fit in.

This is why the opening quote by Robin Sharma speaks to me so much. First off, I admire profound thoughts that come from people who are authentically living their message in a crazy powerful way. Having followed Robin's work for 10 years, I know that everything he does is outside-the-box and comes from a loving place. He's truly an oddball in the most endearing way and this is why he is making his mark on people all across the world. This quote in particular spoke to me because it reminded me in challenging times that the most incredible people on the planet don't fit in. There is nothing about their approach that settles for our society's norm. They embrace being different in the right ways and know that it's necessary to stand out if they are going to create a life that makes the world a cooler place.

I think you will agree with me when I say that there is nothing normal about this approach. I have honestly only seen this type of model authentically lived a few times in my life in person. When you witness authentic "all out" living in person, it's truly remarkable because it almost always results in incredible outcomes for everyone around them. The best example of this for me was my coach Ron. He was a complete oddball in the way he approached coaching. He did things that were so uncommon and wacky that even his athletes who admired him were caught wondering what he was doing on a constant basis. It was this outside-the-box approach that taught us one of the most valuable rules about living we could have ever learned. I wish I would have realized exactly what I was witnessing at the time.

THE QUIRKY RON RULES

When I first started to go to practice at the USA Everett wrestling club, it didn't take me long to realize that there was nothing normal about my coach Ron. He was almost immediately far and away the most unique leader I had ever been around. To start with, he never had us call him coach, Coach Ron or Coach Bessemer. It was just Ron. I think he really liked his name and didn't feel the need to have us call him coach to give him authority. We all knew he was our coach and respected him deeply. Even the way he interacted with us was so different. Whenever I would arrive at practice, he would always ask me about my family and school right away. Once we were done with the "important things," then he would ask if I was ready for training.

In practice, Ron did things that were so completely outside the box. I remember one time he brought in ropes and proceeded to wrap them around our torsos. He asked us kindly with a mischievous smile on his face to keep our arms tightly to our sides as he proceeded to wrap the rope around our biceps. In our training that day, we had to have looked like a bunch of T-Rex babies stalking down our prey. It had to be hysterical for the parents to watch this training exercise. But do you know something fascinating? Ron knew exactly what he was doing because my positioning improved immediately because I learned to keep my elbows tight in Greco-Roman wrestling. I am convinced this is one of the main reasons why I was able to win a few national titles in high school.

There were also the times that he put us through grueling workouts and then asked us to lay down on our backs at the end of practice. He proceeded to instruct us to rest our arms to our sides and to feel our entire body relaxing. This is when Ron would put us through breathing exercises where we inhaled deeply through our noses and exhaled out our mouths. Once he had us in a relaxed state, he instructed us to picture ourselves at the national tournament shaking our opponents hands and feeling completely loose and confident. He proceeded to walk us through the phases of the match until we had pictured ourselves executing and winning it. I now realize that Ron was the first person to actually teach me meditation and active visualization.

We honestly thought Ron was completely nuts at times. But I would be lying if I didn't also say that we absolutely loved it because we were embracing unique in a way that got us incredible results. We also knew that everything we were asked to do was in our best interests because Ron loved us unconditionally and wanted us to succeed. It was this quirky, innovative environment that led me to the best performances of my athletic career. I won three national championships, made three world teams and got a full-athletic scholarship to Indiana University because of an incredible leader who taught me valuable life lessons that I will never forget.

Above all, Ron taught me to strive to have a blast doing what I loved. While other coaches were preaching seriousness and being a tough guy, Ron spoke about excitement, wrestling loose and having fun while competing at the biggest tournaments. I still remember vividly him coming up to me before major national competitions in his leather Harley jacket with a big ole smile on his face and asking, "Are you ready buddy? Let's have some fun today!" In my 20 years of being a competitive athlete, I never had another coach approach the pursuit of goals in this manner. It always had a way of loosening me up so I could go out and just compete the way I was capable of competing. It was so much flippin fun!

Do you want to know something else fascinating about Ron? One of the most powerful lessons I ever learned from him was not one that he actually taught. Let me clarify here. It was never a lesson that he sat down and emphasized in practice. But it was one he modeled at an incredibly high level every single day you were around him. It wasn't any one specific thing that he did. Instead, it was a combination of his abnormal love for his athletes and the wild, outside-the-box training techniques that he brought to practice each day. It was the way he intentionally taught lessons in a sage-like manner at the exact time you needed them. It was the bliss that he brought every single day to training that showed you how to truly love the process.

This is when I realized what made Ron so special. *He was crazy unique!* What made him so memorable was that there was no other coach in the world quite like him. He had a deep desire to push boundaries to find new ways to help his athletes gain an edge and achieve their dreams. Not just on the mat. Ron was passionate about passing on life lessons to every kid so they could be successful outside the practice room. That's when it hit me. He went completely against society's standard of fitting in. He was the antithesis of this model. While the rest of the world was urging you to tone down expectations, he was showing up every single day passionate about helping you find an entirely different level in your life. Ron didn't want you to fit in. He wanted you to pull out your potential so you could STAND OUT.

Reflecting on this remarkable man made me realize that I needed to be far more intentional with my approach. If I was going to become an oddball that changed the world, I was going to have to step up my game. It's one thing to have a powerful dream that you program into your brain. I had now done that for months and it was guiding my daily decisions. It's another thing entirely to be disciplined enough to create a series of daily cues that serve as checkpoints to make the journey successful. I knew that life was far too cluttered to coast into days hoping that my vision would stumble upon me one day.

I had to be way more creative in my approach if I was going to flip the script on my self-doubt and desire to fit in.

It was time to start trying to be a little more odd in my approach.

It was time to channel my inner Ron.

THE MAGIC OF "MOTIVANTRAS"

The value drivers were an incredibly powerful shift because they allowed me to narrow in on focal points that I could pursue daily. No matter what, these were totally under my control every single day. It was always within my power to choose to be more present, giving, curious and gritty. These gave my brain specific outcomes to pursue that would allow me to close the gap on my dreams consistently. Each day I revisited them with emotion, they programmed my brain to be intentional in my most important value areas. It was such an energizing process because the more I emphasized these drivers, the more I became authentic in my daily approach to living.

I was going through my routine one morning when I sensed that I was leaving something on the table with my value drivers. While they were clearly dramatically changing my behaviors and approach to living, there was an entirely different level for them on the horizon that would blow the lid off my potential. You see, I had always loved using motivational mantras to help drive behavior on a daily basis. *Make Your Mark*, the title of my second book, was something I had previously reminded myself to do every single day when interacting with my family, friends and clients. I wanted to be sure to intentionally impact them as much as possible. This simple statement inspired me to take action because it tapped into my passion to influence people's lives in a creative manner. I started to realize that this is the power of motivational mantras, which I now call Motivantras, when used properly.

What if I connected a meaningful Motivantra to each of my value drivers? I pondered. *What if I could take the power of my most important drivers and connect them to a themed mantra that inspires me to take bigger action in my life?*

I was intrigued by the idea so I wrote down some of my favorite mantras that I had previously used on a daily basis to inspire action. I immediately thought of mantras like *Make Moments, Earn the Right* and *BRING the BLISS.* They got me fired up just thinking about them and how they had inspired me to live at a higher level over the previous six months. I took each of the mantras and attached them to a value driver. My initial list immediately piqued my interest and looked like the following.

Present → Make Moments

Giving → Speak Life

ENERGY → Be a Charger

Passion → Bring the Bliss

Curious → Give and Grow

Grateful → Find the Gift

As I looked them over, I found myself intrigued and inspired by their potential right away. I knew the power of Motivantras when used properly to drive your behavior. I couldn't help but think about how much stronger they would be when tied to drivers specifically designed to close the gap on my value visions. *What if I added these to the mix in my morning routine and then connected them to Sacred Space time frames during my days?* I pondered. I was immediately captivated by the idea so I decided to give it a run starting the next morning.

The first time I added these Motivantras to my routine, it was an absolute game changer for me. I knew I wanted to be more passionate in my approach, but *BRING the BLISS* took things to an entirely different level. It inspired me to move into my key roles with an entirely different level of focus. I didn't want to just exist. I wanted to bring a dynamic approach that inspired the people around me to find an entirely different level in their lives. Of course I wanted to be more present in my most important roles, but it was *Make Moments* that reminded me to lock in and create special memories with my family, friends and clients. The same thing happened with every single one of my value drivers. The Motivantras were like boosters that launched each of them into another stratosphere.

It makes complete sense when you stop and think about it. Creating a powerful vision in your most important life areas is a transformational process. It piques your brain's interest and gives you a framework of what you would like to ultimately achieve in life. Then you come along and breathe life into the entire process by creating value drivers that give you an initial roadmap to realize your vision. This is the part where you increase your inspiration fuel tank because you start to realize the person you are truly passionate about becoming in your life. The Motivantras are simply the boosters because they take an already charged process and ignite it into something filled with a unique desire to be different.

It's interesting how much your approach changes when you stop waiting for your goals to show up at your doorstep. There is something magical that happens the moment you begin to actively seek out ways to close the gap on your goals. I am convinced that the most powerful way to make this happen is by considering the person you need and desire to become to EARN your vision. This step is so transformational because it gives you far more than just instructions on how to close the gap on your goals. It gives you a blueprint on how to live your life with real purpose each and every day. When you know the person you are passionate about becoming, it gives you something tangible and meaningful to pursue at all times.

CALLING ALL CRITICISM THAT COMES WITH CRAZY UNIQUE

Before we transition into the final phase of how to be crazy unique in your approach, we need to address a barrier that comes with the territory when you strive to stand out in your life. It's one thing to get excited about the idea of shunning the status quo while reading this book in the safety and comfort of your own home. It's another thing entirely to authentically practice it when your environment doesn't cooperate.

Here's a fact you need to accept and embrace:

Your environment will challenge you when you step up and commit to living to your highest potential.

Why? Because the moment you commit to being completely and unapologetically you, it means you are different. You have chosen to rock the boat. If there is one thing I have learned from my journey, it is that there is definitely a cost that you must be willing to pay if you are going to be unique in the way you live your life.

I still remember when my second book *Make Your Mark* was released. It had an incredible amount of positive ENERGY around the launch and there was so much encouraging feedback about how it was helping people elevate their lives. I was naturally excited about all of this because it meant that my work was making an impact on people's lives in the way that I had hoped that it would. I was scrolling through emails from readers one day when I stumbled upon one with an interesting subject line. It read "In case you were wondering." I was curious so I immediately clicked on it to give it a read. I quickly realized that this was not going to be another supportive, "pat you on the back" email. Instead, I was immediately greeted by a blunt man who was eager to share his sharp criticism about my book.

Dear Coyte,

I recently read a part of your Make Your Mark book because it had been recommended by a friend of mine who really loved it. I decided that it was worth a shot so I borrowed their copy. I started reading the book immediately and found myself very disappointed because it just didn't deliver. I found it to be quite unrealistic in its approach and did not think that your philosophy would work. It was honestly a waste of my time. I felt it necessary to share my honest feedback with you. I hope it is useful. I am happy to share more feedback about my philosophy if you are interested.

Sincerely,

Paul

I wish I could tell you that I completely blew this message off. In an ideal world, I could share with you right now how I handled it with grace by balancing this one scathing review with the slew of glowing feedback I had received. Honestly, I didn't do this at all. Instead, I allowed the reader's comments to get in and penetrate my beliefs. I immediately found myself questioning my work and feeling guilty that it had not met the reader's expectations. I replied hoping I could find a way to make it right for him. I now realize it was never my job to please this reader.

One of the things that helped me flip the script on criticism was listening to a talk by Rachel Hollis, the author of *Girl, Wash Your Face*. She was smack dab in the middle of a powerful segment on building a thriving business when she arrived at the topic of criticism. After opening up about instances when she allowed it to negatively impact her, Rachel introduced a topic that she now embraces to keep her work authentic and impactful. I was honestly immediately drawn in when she passionately explained to the audience, "If you aren't in the arena actually doing battle with me, then you don't get the right to criticize my work. I refuse to give people in the cheap sets an opinion on how I am living my life. I reserve this for the people who are with me on a daily basis and understand what it takes to do what I do."

This was such a profound realization for me. I recognized right then that I still had the wrong perspective about my work. It wasn't my job to please everyone. That was an impossible task to accomplish anyways because somebody was always going to have an opinion. My sole purpose as an author, coach and speaker is to pour my heart and soul into work that truly matters to me. It is to do everything in my power to create messages that empower people to live to their highest potential. If I do this to the best of my ability with every product I release, then I have done my job. I can definitely live with any criticism that comes at this point. Once you have shown up every day, and fought and earned the right to build the lifestyle you have dreamed of, you will feel this way too.

THE FLIP FROM FIT IN TO STAND OUT

I was sorting through all of this fitting in and self-doubt stuff one day when the solution to my problem hit me.

I was the cause of my own pain.

It's not an easy pill to swallow when you realize it, but I have learned to embrace it because it means that I also have the solution to my problem. Even as I reflected on this process and embraced my new Motivantras, I still had moments when I was worried about fitting in. I think this is reasonable because it can take some time to shake this programming out given it has often been with us most of our lives. The difference was that I now realized what was at stake.

Do you know where self-doubt comes from? Yeah, I agree that it often stems from past situations when we have been rejected and told in one way or another that we are not enough. But what writing this chapter taught me is that this is not actually the root cause. That comes from our core desire to fit in. As long as we need to be accepted, we will always look to others to tell us that we are enough. Nothing will change here unless we shift our programming. *Not fit in, STAND OUT.* We must embrace being different if we are going to flip the script on self-doubt. Criticism will always be a part of life, but it doesn't have to impact our self-worth. The moment we embrace being an oddball and standing out to our core, the past situations that have caused us the greatest pains can actually magically transform into moments that inspire us to our highest potential.

I now understood that the key to flipping the script on my self-doubt was to strive to STAND OUT. The cool thing was that I had everything I needed to make that happen. I just had to work the system that I now had in place with a passion so I could be extraordinary in my most important value areas.

No more fitting in, Coyte. Enough already!

Just get out and embrace your Motivantras so you can close the gap on your goals!

Bring the Bliss!

Make Moments!

EARN the Right!

It was this simple mindset shift that started to pull out my potential and allowed me to be completely unique in my approach.

FLIPPIN FITTING IN

When the high ranking administrator at the university first told me that I was a "really good baseball player, but that I was playing cricket," I saw it entirely the wrong way. I immediately processed it and thought about all the ways I had not been enough. It frustrated me that I was not an adequate cricket player deserving of making the team. I now realize that my biggest barrier at the time was being worried about fitting in and pleasing others because it caused me to miss the point entirely. You see, in the middle of this seemingly meaningless comment was a profound message with the potential to radically transform my life. I just needed a perspective shift to finally recognize it for what is was.

Do you know the interesting thing? I now believe that this administrator was exactly right and I have no hard feelings about it whatsoever. I didn't belong at the university. The truth is that the skill sets that I brought to the table weren't quite enough to be there. The only difference now is that I see this as a point of pride. Why? Because he was right that I was not a cricket player. And honestly, I never was going to be. Instead, I am meant to be out right now doing exactly what I am doing on my own terms. I never would have been able to take this journey, write this book and find myself if I had never been told that I wasn't the right fit at the university. Learning that I didn't fit in, while painful at the time, provided me with a gift to eventually find a path that has allowed me to stand out.

If you have areas of your life where you are trying too hard to fit in, I hope you are sick of it. There is nothing more frustrating than working hard to be accepted only to be constantly rejected or pushed to the side. You don't deserve that.

You deserve to know what it feels like to actually go out and pursue the things you are passionate about all out.

You deserve to have the opportunity to experience what it is like to become the person you have always felt you are capable of becoming.

You deserve to get the chance to feel the joy that comes when you are living life on your own terms and using your gifts to pursue your passions.

YELLOW BALL #6
THE "EMOTIONAL MOTIVANTRA" HABIT

We will keep this one simple. The desire to fit in stinks. Especially when it is costing you your ability to go out and live the life you are capable of living. If we are going to swap this out, we need to give your brain a much better option that instead allows you to stand out in your own unique way. To make this happen, we need to identify the person that you are passionate about becoming in the future.

I hope you are uber excited to get to work because this is a transformational activity. All you need to do initially is identify two to three value drivers that will help you close the gap on your top value visions. Once you have them in place, push to find an associated Motivantra for these value drivers that will inspire you to be extraordinary in your life. After this, you know the drill. Commit to seeing, hearing and feeling them every single day during your morning routine so you can program your brain to pursue them all out. Then use them throughout your day in important "Sacred Space" time periods to drive your performance to an entirely different level.

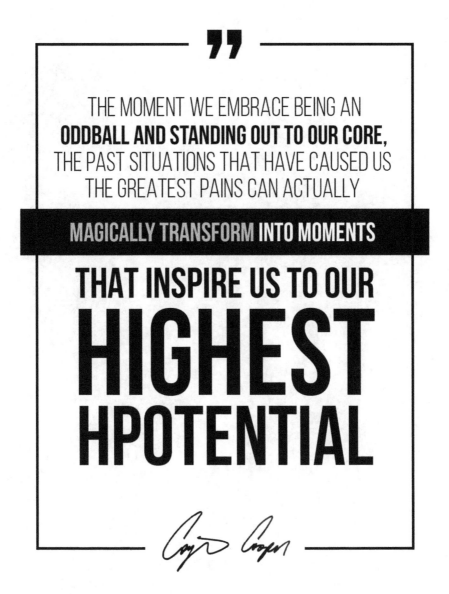

"

THE MOMENT WE EMBRACE BEING AN
ODDBALL AND STANDING OUT TO OUR CORE,
THE PAST SITUATIONS THAT HAVE CAUSED US
THE GREATEST PAINS CAN ACTUALLY

MAGICALLY TRANSFORM INTO MOMENTS

THAT INSPIRE US TO OUR
HIGHEST
HPOTENTIAL

CHAPTER 7

OBLIGATION

NOT HAVE TO...BLESSED TO

*"Working hard for something we don't care about is called stress.
Working hard for something we love is called passion."*
—Simon Sinek

I pulled into my driveway after a long, six-hour day of travel. I had been on the road the last couple days giving keynote talks across the state in Eastern Washington. I had poured into creating dynamic experiences and my brain was feeling a little worn down. I headed into my house and was immediately greeted enthusiastically by my two kids Carter and Mya and our Siberian Husky Kira. After embracing them all, I headed over to my wife Brandy to give her a big hug. It was nice to be home. I quickly transitioned to checking my email where I had a couple of messages I needed to respond to. Just as I hit the reply button to craft my first response, my son Carter came up and tapped me on the shoulder and asked softly, "Do you want to play dinosaurs?" I paused for a moment as my immediate default response was that I honestly didn't because I was tired. I had been on the road all day long and just wanted to relax for a few minutes. I am not proud of it now, but I told him "maybe later buddy."

I can't tell you how many times this has likely been my default response in the past. It doesn't make me particularly pleased to admit it, but it's the honest truth. In the midst of the clutter of living, I have had many moments when I forget what is truly important to me. When this happens, I tend to neglect my value visions and fall short of who I am capable of being as a human being. The same thing has happened in my work. Have I always wanted to write this book since the day I started it? *Nah, not really.* There were so many times early on when I didn't feel like it and put it off until later in the day. I am guessing you can relate when reflecting on the most important things in your own life.

The problem with this approach is that it often continues to result in putting your most important things off a little longer. We totally intend to make them happen at some point, but then life keeps showing up giving us reasons to avoid doing the exact things we know we should be doing. If my personal and coaching experiences are anything remotely close to being representative of the norm, then later tends to never actually arrive or it is few and far between. I have found that this is the subtle space where mundane creeps in and robs us of the opportunity to make our life truly remarkable and memorable.

The other response that has become a common pattern for me at times is following through on my intentions because I "have to." With this approach, I do tend to get it done, but it also feels an awful lot like an unpleasant obligation. If there is anything I have learned during this process, it's that our brain doesn't like obligation because it is often associated with pain. The fascinating thing is that I have often patted myself on the back in the past when following through on my intentions in these instances. Listen, learning to do your most important things even when you don't feel like it is a master skill set. But if we are always miserable doing them, I believe that we have missed the point entirely. There can and should be joy in the process.

As I sat reflecting on these areas where I had fallen short, I started to ask myself some revealing questions:

How did I arrive at this point?

Why is it that it's so easy to neglect your most important things?

This is when it hit me. I had taken them for granted. In the middle of the busyness of everyday life, I had consistent moments each day when I got so distracted that I forgot why my most important roles were so important to me. This is exactly when I had adopted a habit that is quite common in our society. It happens to be one that is robbing most people daily of the ability to be great in their lives. I finally realized that my issue is that I had started to coast in the key areas of my life.

COASTING IS ACTUALLY QUITE COMMON

First off, let's outline exactly what it means to coast. To me, coasting is what happens when you start to go through the motions. It's that spot in life where you get so busy that you start to forget what truly matters to you. This is so common in our society where we are constantly barraged with thousands of messages via 24/7 technology access. The other path to coasting comes when things are going pretty solid so you subtly decide to put it on autopilot. Either way, the end result is that you start coasting and miss out on areas where you could really excel and make your life memorable.

How do I know so much about coasting? Well, when I got honest with myself, I realized that I was a bit of a "coaster." Now, I'm pretty sure that nobody who knows me well would actually describe me this way. I am guessing that the people closest to me would say that I am a passionate person who consistently strives to live to potential in my life. But that wouldn't be completely accurate. You see, the truth is that I coasted as an NCAA scholarship athlete. I also coasted as a college professor at a premier academic institution. I have coasted at times as a parent and husband. If I am being completely straight with you, I have coasted in every single role and goal that has ever mattered to me.

Not all the time of course. In every one of these situations, there were times when I was crystal clear on exactly who I wanted to be and CRUSHED IT in the key areas of my life. However, these times tended to be more of the exception than the norm because I had not yet learned to be highly intentional with my approach. When life got really hectic, I found myself wandering off track and going through the motions. I was not doing a terrible job because I was still showing up and giving a decent effort. The problem is that decent just doesn't cut it when you want to create results you are truly proud of. If you are a driven person, decent always morphs into disappointment when you are performing below potential in the areas of your life that matter to you most.

Do you know what I realized during my journey? I'm not alone here. The honest truth is that coasting is quite common in our society. Not just with your average every day person. It actually turns out this has been a universal trend with pretty much every proactive person I have worked with in my life. Don't get me wrong. I am certainly not saying they were being completely lazy because the reality is that many of them were operating in prominent leadership positions. They were achieving at a high level based on societal standards. But they also weren't performing near their potential in the key areas of their lives. Why? They had gotten to the point where they were so busy that they had lost track of the engine driving excellence in their lives.

When you look up coasting via Google, Wikipedia defines it as "a natural deceleration of a motor when the power is removed." When I first read this definition, I thought to myself: *Yes, that's it exactly! That's exactly what has happened in my own life!* It turns out that this is what had happened in my clients' lives as well. We had lost track of the core ENERGY source driving our passion and purpose on a daily basis. I realized quickly that this was the primary reason why I had started to coast in the key areas of my life.

IT'S NO WONDER WITHOUT A WHY

So, why do people coast and allow this to happen? Wait, hold up. Let me ask that a different way with less ego. *Why have I coasted at times in the past and fell short of expectations?* These were two versions of the same question that I asked myself literally dozens of times while writing this chapter. The more I asked it with emotional intensity, the more the universe seemed to deliver me the answers I was seeking. The first insightful thought that came to me was in the form of intention. It became clear rather quickly that most people don't actually sit down and make a conscious decision to neglect the things that matter to them most. Certainly not the type of people who are reading this book. I think the process is far subtler and often occurs without people even knowing it.

The second insightful intuition arrived when I realized that all of the coasting examples I had considered had one thing in common. They were all missing a key ingredient when it came to living with intention and passion. I realized I was no different in this way. *How did I allow myself to become a coaster?* Like most people, I got caught up in the clutter of day-to-day living and lost track of the main reasons WHY I was so passionate about pursuing my value visions. I had lost my power source and was decelerating without even realizing it.

In college, I had gotten so wrapped up in training that I forgot entirely why I loved wrestling and the opportunity to compete at an elite NCAA level that stretched my potential. As a professor, I was so busy striving to get tenure that I lost track of how incredible it was to have the chance to work with remarkably talented students in the classroom. As a husband and parent, I somehow allowed the busyness of living to distract me from the extraordinary gift I had each day to love my family unconditionally and make moments with them.

In hindsight, it's no wonder why my clients and I were falling into the trap of coasting in our lives. We had lost track of the reasons WHY we were so passionate about pursuing our value visions in the first place. We didn't have a clear, compelling reason to show up and continue to fight for the things that mattered to us most. I decided instantly that I was no longer willing to coast anymore. I didn't want mundane to become my norm. If it was an option, and I believed it was, I wanted magical in the life areas that mattered to me most. I wanted to know for certain that I was flat out using it up every single day. If this was going to happen, it was time to tap into WHY and flip the script on coast mode.

WHY NOT ME? AND WHY NOT YOU?

I was sitting at my desk writing this chapter when a Russell Wilson quote popped into my mind: *"Why not me? Why not you? Why not us? Why not now? Why not try?"* I absolutely love this quote because Russell Wilson is a crazy passionate human being who has completely disregarded the odds on his journey to becoming a premier quarterback in the National Football League (NFL). It also triggers an emotional response that makes me want to blast through a brick wall so I can close the gap on my goals.

This time the quote hit me from a completely different angle. It immediately put me in a curious state where I was fixated on understanding the exact reasons so many people are falling short of expectations. I knew that a large part of this had to do with people not having a strong "WHY" to drive their behaviors, but I wondered how we arrived at this particular destination where we are perpetually disappointed and living well below our potential. This helped me realize that there is more than one way to fall into a routine where we are going through the motions.

Chasing the Wrong Things. There is one guaranteed way to eventually coast in your life. It is actually a route that has become quite common because of the tremendous pressure our society tends to have on our preferences and decisions. There are literally thousands of messages each day surrounding us that encourage pursuing attention, money and status. There is nothing necessarily wrong with wanting these things. When kept in perspective, these are areas that can increase the quality of your life. That is, if they matter to you. The problem is that people prioritize things like this and it causes them to pursue the wrong things for the wrong reasons.

This inevitably leads them down a path where they arrive at one of two undesirable outcomes. The most common result is that you struggle to reach your desired end outcome because you lack a passion for the thing you are pursuing. When it doesn't matter enough, you will rarely fight to earn the right to achieve something. The second outcome that can occur is that you close the gap on the outcome you are pursuing, but you arrive at your end destination and it still feels empty. This is often what happens when you chase after things that don't fit your values. Not you or me, though. We are ready to flip the script on this one because we already have our value visions in place!

Chasing the Right Things. This just doesn't make sense, does it? How can chasing the right things lead to coasting and settling your life? The gut response answer is that it really doesn't. In fact, chasing the right things happens to be the best way to radically increase the level of passion and vibrancy you experience in your life. It is one of the most satisfying feelings in the world to know you are progressing towards things you are meant to be doing. Yet this is an experience that is dodging millions of well-intentioned people across the United States and world. They are operating in the right roles, but they still find themselves feeling underwhelmed with their results and lives.

How is this possible? I mean they are pursuing the right things so passion should come naturally, right? WRONG. The truth is that you can have extraordinary opportunities in front of you, but they can also easily get lost in the crazy clutter of day-to-day living. It's entirely possible for your most important things to turn into obligations that make life mundane if you are not intentional with your approach. The truth is that this concept is just too important to blow past in a single paragraph. It deserves an entire section because it holds one of the secrets to living a life that is full of passion and purpose.

WHEN LOVE TURNS INTO LABOR

At the start of the chapter, I led with an incredible quote by Simon Sinek that sparked the seed thought for this entire chapter. Let's unpack it a little.

I think we can all agree that choosing the wrong things tends to lead to stress because it means grinding away at activities that don't intrigue or inspire our soul. I'm guessing you can relate here because everyone has made a decision to pursue something for the wrong reasons at some point in their lives. We often feel restless because it seems like something is always missing no matter how hard we work. This is frustrating. However, this isn't the only way to arrive at a place where you feel unfulfilled. There happens to be a far sneakier culprit here that robs us of the ability to have passion and purpose in our lives. The interesting thing is that we rarely see it coming and often don't even realize it is even occurring as we move through our day-to-day lives.

When things are new, they tend to come easier. Our brain gets excited by intriguing stimuli and this often results in ENERGY coming more naturally when we first begin something that matters to us. We see this play out regularly in the different phases of our life. It's exciting when you start a new relationship with someone special. It's exciting when you experience the invigoration of beginning a new business. It's exciting when you take a risk and go out to pursue your dreams. This excitement generally means you are more likely to pour into these things because they are invigorating. There is something about newness that pulls out our enthusiasm and intention.

Then the newness starts to wear off and that initial passion we had is harder to come by. As this occurs, the busyness of life starts to occupy our attention and that thing we love slowly and subtly gets pushed off to the side little by little. Eventually, we get so caught up in the stimuli of our day-to-day clutter that we completely lose track of the reasons why these things were so important to us in the first place. This is the exact moment when opportunity starts to turn into obligation. Without realizing it, the thing we once loved has now turned into labor that brings stress into our lives.

If you don't believe it, then just pay attention to how you interact with the most important people and things in your life. It is likely that there are instances every single week where you treat them like an obligation if you are not intentional with your approach. When I first thought about this concept, it absolutely blew my mind because I realized I was doing this in every single one of my top three value areas. It was at this exact moment that I started to grasp the profound implications of my actions if I didn't change how I was approaching living my days. The thing that moved me most was recognizing that it's totally possible for the thing I love to become disappointing. It actually happens all the time.

The marriage that was once passionate becomes boring.

The kids that were once your purpose become a nuisance.

The career that once seemed like your calling has morphed into a mundane mandatory exercise.

The crazy thing is that we accept this as being completely normal. People tell us that this is just the way it is and we take it to the bank as being a fact. *It's just the normal ebb and flow of life.* The only problem is that this is utterly false. There is no rule that says you have to lose passion for the things that matter to you most. In fact, it is totally possible for the exact opposite to occur in your life. If you are disciplined in your daily approach to living, you can build a deep passion that charges your life and drives your behaviors on a consistent daily basis. When I realized this, it was an absolute game changer for me.

WHY IS WHERE YOUR FIGHT COMES FROM

I want to reiterate something just in case you missed it the first time. Passion and purpose are NEVER going to just show up at your doorstep promising to make your life simple. I don't care what the movies tell you. This just isn't the way that life works. We have already discussed how it tends to flow naturally when things are new. On the flip side, there is also a point when this newness wears off and passion wanes. That is, if you don't have habits in place to sustain and elevate it. This is why it's so important that you continue to reinforce a mindset that encourages you to fight for the things that matter to you most. *Not easy, EARN IT,* remember?

Now that you are getting familiar with the things that matter to you most, it is time to train your brain to focus on WHY you love them so much. Make it a priority to light your mind up with excitement for your vision daily so it knows how important it is to you. Never leave your most important values and outcomes to chance in your life. Once this becomes your habit, it will pull out purpose that drives intention in your days. Rather than backing off and coasting, you will feel an inspiring urge within you to start fighting more for the end destinations and outcomes you desire.

This might be one of the most important lessons in the book. In a world that is urging us to expect instant, step up and connect with your WHY so you are ready to fight for the things that matter to you most in life. Remind yourself daily of the reasons you are committed to showing up so you start to see your value visions as an opportunity. One of the most dynamic, tangible transformations I observe when people embrace this philosophy is how they perceive "unreasonable" investments. It seems unreasonable to get up at 5:00am to invest in yourself, right? Lots of normal people believe this to be true, but it isn't quite accurate. Not when you realize how much it helps you cultivate clarity and a confidence in your ability to close the gap on your goals.

I have never met a person who fully embraced the morning growth routine over an extended time period that regretted it. Instead, the most incredible thing often happens. The same people who initially labeled themselves as "not morning people" eventually see it as a must and start referring to themselves as "early risers." Why? There is something magical that happens when you start to show up and fight for the things that truly matter to you most. Are there mornings when you don't feel like getting out of bed? Of course! The only difference now is you have a reason to get to bed and that starts to drive your daily decisions and behaviors.

The take home lesson here is that your WHY will bring your fight out.

Why should I put my phone down and spend time with my kids?

Because I want to be a remarkable parent who loves my kids unconditionally and makes incredible moments with them. That's WHY!

Why should I lock in and embrace writing this chapter when I don't feel like it?

Because it will allow me to EARN the right to release a book that inspires readers deeply to scrap to pull out their highest potential. That's WHY!

Why should I get up every single morning and listen to a song that reminds me to pursue passion in my marriage?

Because I want to create a deep relationship with my wife that makes our life an incredible journey. That's WHY!

Eventually, if you remind yourself WHY often enough, the fight you bring to your day will become your norm and it will lead you to an extraordinary place in your life.

THE FLIP FROM "HAVE TO" TO "BLESSED TO"

Let's take a trip back to that moment when my son Carter came up to me and asked me to play dinosaurs. I think we can both agree that if family is my top value and I am committed to making moments with them, I can do much better. This is especially true when I have been on the road and my kids haven't seen me for a couple of days. But honestly, it can be challenging to be present enough in the moment to be authentic to your vision. I learned a few different strategies that really helped me step up in my role as a parent. These were the steps that I took to flip the script on obligation so I could start seeing my top values for what they are, blessings. They were "Sacred Space" moments and it was time to start treating them that way.

The first step that I took was to start programming my brain to see my most important roles as opportunities. As I went through my morning routine, I made a point to remind myself that I was blessed to get to be my kid's father. It wasn't something I "had to" do. It was something I "got to" do. *No, check that.* I was "blessed to" be able to do it. This small shift may seem inconsequential, but it's actually a powerful shift when you are trying to get your brain to stop looking at your most important things as obligation. Each time you remind yourself that you are blessed to be alive pursuing extraordinary in your top value areas, it reinforces to your brain the incredible opportunity you have in front of you.

The second thing I started to do each day that ended up being really transformational was to stop and experience the core blessings in my life. I would pause intentionally at least once a day and look at my kids and wife with the sole intention of feeling overwhelming gratitude for them. The morning blessed bank had primed me for this exercise. I did the same thing in my work and it changed the way I saw it entirely. It was so profound to notice how this perspective shift elevated my effectiveness and overall quality of life. But do you know something interesting? I still had moments when I found the "have to" mentality creeping in during key moments in my day. I realized that I needed one final strategy to flip the script on obligation when these times came.

Here is the exact strategy that I created to finally turn obligation into opportunity. This became a Houdini act that I used to put an end to the curse that is coasting. It is actually pretty simple, but I learned that it can totally take mundane and turn it into magical if you embrace it with a sense of curiosity and excitement. I think I will just walk you through the steps as if I was using them in real time. Now imagine my little man Carter walking up to me that day and asking me to play dinosaurs. This is exactly what I did to flip the script on obligation and to turn my "have to" into "blessed to."

1. **Release "have to" thoughts and "not feeling like it"** – I learned that the first step to creating change here is to recognize the moments when the "have to" mentality starts creeping in. If you don't know when they are happening, you really can't do anything about them. This is not extremely difficult with the right approach. Since you know your top value areas, it's really about paying attention to your attitude towards them when you

move into "Sacred Space" time frames. When you start to realize the voice creeping in telling you that you don't feel like it, just don't respond to it and instead make the decision to release it.

2. **Redirect to "blessed to" and connect to your role** – Once you have learned not to pay attention to your initial "have to" response, it's really as simple as giving your brain a better option. Rather than continuing to allow the obligation mentality to creep in, remind yourself that you are blessed to be in this role and redirect your mind to the vision that you are passionate about pursuing. I have found it really helpful to come back to the exact things that I revisit in my morning routine. If you have been working the process, these will be anchored so you will be ready to program your brain in real time with these powerful options.

3. **Reinforce with top Motivantra** – This final step was an absolute game changer for me. Once I had reconnected to my vision and had started to redirect my brain to a "blessed to" perspective point, I reinforced this entire process with a powerful Motivantra. In this instance, I simply reminded myself to *Make Moments* that my kids would always remember. If I felt like I needed an ENERGY boost, I would urge myself to *Bring the Bliss*. Because these were statements that inspired me and I had been programming them into my brain each morning, they were areas of emphasis that gave me a boost that allowed me to fully embrace the opportunities in front of me.

There is one final step you need to make to fully flip the script on obligation. You need to be disciplined about rinsing and repeating it until you feel a full on "blessed to" mentality spilling over into every part of your life. This one is totally worth pursuing because it will completely elevate your approach to living and the quality of emotions that you experience. There will certainly be times when it's difficult, but if you keep showing up and fight for it, eventually the feeling of gratitude and appreciation will flood your brain and life. Equally important, you will start to really embrace the opportunity to bring the best of yourself to your most important times in your day.

FLIPPIN OBLIGATION

Honestly, change happened for me when I finally noticed that I was coasting in the key areas of my life. It's strange how you can adjust your life's path almost immediately when you are honest about areas where you are falling short of potential. The biggest thing for me is that I wasn't willing to allow my family, career and vitality to become an obligation. Instead, I wanted to see them as an opportunity. I knew for a fact that I could never experience the vibrant life I desired if I was walking around seeing my top values as something I "had to" do. The only way I could ever live to potential is if I learned to see them as an absolute blessing. The moment that this happened, my entire life transformed because I started to approach my top value areas with the time, ENERGY and positive expectations that they deserved.

Are you tired of feeling like you are going through the motions at times in your life? Do you want to know that you are using it up every single day in the value areas that are most important to you? If so, then refuse to continue to see them as an obligation. They aren't something you "have to" do. They are incredible opportunities that you are "blessed to" have in your life every single day. Commit to working the steps outlined in this chapter until you start to experience a profound sense of gratitude for them. You are totally capable of extraordinary in your life. But only if you step up and give your most important value areas the respect they deserve.

YELLOW BALL #7

THE "BLESSED TO" HABIT

It's time to change the dirty diaper that is obligation. You already know that it's stinking up your life so it's time to let it go. If we are going to make that happen, it's important that you start reminding yourself what a true blessing your top value areas are during your morning routine. Once you have done this, make a push to go into your sacred space time slots each day and remind yourself to see them as an incredible opportunity. Then all you have to do once you have built momentum is to start working the "4 R's" when you sense the obligation mentality creeping in during your day. This is when you can work on (1) releasing the "have to" mentality, (2) redirecting to the "blessed to" philosophy and (3) reinforcing it all with a powerful Motivantra. Remember, keep (4) rinsing and repeating all of these steps until you start to move into your roles with a passion to be truly great in them.

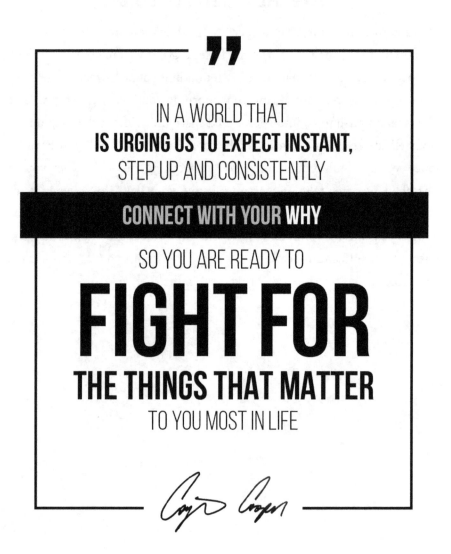

"

IN A WORLD THAT
IS URGING US TO EXPECT INSTANT,
STEP UP AND CONSISTENTLY

CONNECT WITH YOUR WHY

SO YOU ARE READY TO

FIGHT FOR

THE THINGS THAT MATTER
TO YOU MOST IN LIFE

CHAPTER 8

NOT PRESENT

MAKE MOMENTS...THAT ARE REMARKABLE AND MEMORABLE

"Life is a series of moments. The quality of attention and action that we bring to each moment determines the quality of our lives."
—Dan Millman

It was a beautiful summer afternoon and I was sitting in the kitchen visiting with my wife Brandy. We were talking about this book and the topic of living intentionally came up. I could tell that something was definitely on her mind so I asked her, "What's up, B?" She pondered for a moment as she looked down at our white marble countertops. After a few seconds, she lifted her head up and had a serious look in her eyes as she responded, "I don't feel like I am doing a very good job parenting our kids. I don't feel like I am doing near enough." I have to admit that this statement caught me completely off guard. I honestly initially had no idea how to respond because my wife is an incredible mother. Fortunately, a few seconds later, a brilliant thought popped into my mind. I walked over to the kitchen area designated for our kids' school stuff. I gathered a stack of Sticky Notes and plopped them right in front of her.

I know what you might be thinking. *Sticky Notes...but why, Coyte?* I'll tell you exactly why. Every single day since Carter started to go to school, Brandy has written him an inspirational, loving note in his lunch. So every time he opens his lunch box to eat, he is greeted by an empowering message that shows him how much he is loved.

You make the world more AWESOME!

You are SUPER DUPER amazing, talented, a go getter!

Don't let anything stand in your way!

Always speak life to yourself and others!

This isn't something that happens occasionally. It happens every single day no matter what. It doesn't matter if Brandy doesn't feel like it. She wants him to know how special he is so she shows up and strives to make moments in his life.

The skeptic here might think, *That's great, Coyte, but how do you know that this is even making a difference? How do you know that this is actually making moments like you say?* I have a response for that as well. I know with 100 percent certainty that it is impacting our little man's life because of the reaction that resulted from it. About 100 days into the school year, Carter started to do something back each day. On every single note, he would write a message back to his mom.

You are AMAZING two mom!

You can get your dreams two!

You are a go getter two mom!

No, I didn't misspell "too" here. Our little man's grammar wasn't quite up to par yet, but he was in first grade so we looked past that part. It was the thought that counted in our minds.

Why does this matter so much? You see, we often think that we need to come up with a well-planned, over-the-top vacation to make moments with the people that matter to us most. While that is certainly one way to do it (*and would likely be a TON of fun!*), I am not convinced that this is truly how you make the most memorable moments in life. Instead, these tend to come from the day-to-day investments we bring to the table when we are intentional about making people's lives special. As I look back on my lifespan, the most memorable experiences came when someone special poured into my life and helped me believe in myself. It was these "smaller" moments that pulled out my potential.

The point is that you don't need to be anything you aren't to make moments in your life. It's not out of your reach. You just need to think about how to make the people's lives close to you special on a consistent basis and then have the toughness to show up daily to make it happen. Will they always notice? Of course not! But if you keep doing it, the investments will eventually add up and turn into something remarkable. This is why we *Bring the Bliss* in our family by dancing wildly to music as a tribe every single night. It is goofy as all get out, but we have a blast together and I know that my kids will remember this habit when they get older. This was Brandy's idea, by the way.

If you truly want to create a life that is memorable, then remind yourself that little things done over and over with passion are what makes life special. When you get up each morning and pour into your family with a great attitude, *you are making moments*. In the times when you write friends to tell them how special they are, *you are making moments*. When you step up and pursue your passion all out without worrying about what critics will say, then *you are definitely making moments*. Why? Because there are people watching who are looking for permission to pursue their own dreams all out. You give them that consent when you cut loose and make no apologies for chasing down the dreams in your heart.

THE MOMMY MOMENT MAKER

My wife is a "Mommy Moment Maker." She doesn't know it yet and would never call herself this, but it's totally the truth. You see, she doesn't just show up and write notes every single day for our little man. This momma shows up on a consistent daily basis and does pretty much everything in her power to make our kids' lives better. I always joke that she would literally starve before our kids got a smidge hungry. I have to admit that it is only half-joking because she loves them that much. It is engrained in every fiber of her being to do what is necessary to make moments in their lives.

Most of it isn't glamorous. Just the other night, our sweet little girl Mya was sick and was in the bathroom pretty much on the hour throughout the entire night. Do you know who was present for every single trip? *BINGO!* Brandy was there for every moment rubbing her precious little back and telling her how much she loved her. I have learned this about my wife. She wants to be there for as many moments as she possibly can because it matters so much to her that they know how much she loves them. Will they remember all of this? Nah, definitely not. They won't remember every single trip to the bathroom she makes with them. But it will undeniably add up and turn into something truly remarkable and memorable someday.

What I am convinced of is that they will remember the fact that she always loved them unconditionally growing up. They will never doubt the way that their mother feels about them. Why? Because she shows up every single day and finds "little" ways to make their life special. It is within the walls of our house where nobody really knows that it's even happening. However, our kids will know and that is what truly matters. Making moments isn't about getting credit. It's about showing up and doing whatever it takes to make people's lives special. This is why my wife Brandy is a "Mommy Moment Maker" and always will be.

Why do I tell you this? First, I honestly wanted to brag on my wife! Brandy is without question one of the humblest, down-to-earth people I have ever met. Never in a million years would she ever tell you the things she does for her kids on a consistent daily basis. Honestly, I don't even believe she thinks it's a thing. It's just what she believes everyone should be doing. Second, I wanted to point out the fact that making moments is something that anyone can do in the roles that matter to them most. It's about stepping up and making it a priority so you don't miss the opportunity.

Maybe you aren't a parent so you don't quite connect with what I am saying here. Don't miss the point because this applies to every person on the planet. If people are important to you, then it's necessary that you learn to step up and embrace the moments that you are given each day. It is in these moments that you have the opportunity to do things that make people's lives so much better. In the process, it is these types of actions that will make your own life remarkable and memorable. THAT is worth fighting for.

I WANT TO BE A MOMENT MAKER TOO!!!

As I reflected on my wife Brandy's approach to parenting, I started to realize that I wanted to be more like her. No, "Mommy Moment Maker" was not in the cards for me, but I definitely wanted to do my own version of this as a father. I was passionate about being far more intentional about stepping up and making sure that my kiddos knew how crazy I was about them. I also wanted to do more things to show my wife Brandy that I loved her unconditionally and believed in her with all my heart. I was passionate about flat out making moments that would be remarkable and memorable for the three most important people in my life.

It seems like a mundane shift, but it made such a monumental transformation in my daily approach to living. As I revisited my value visions with the *Make Moments* emphasis in mind, it primed me to be far more present throughout my days. This led me to locking in on creating memories when playing with my kids. With this focal point, I was far more likely to stop and enjoy playing Life and Uno with them. It turns out that this is still a flippin blast when you are 38-years old rocking the right mindset. This ended up being such a blessing because it allowed me to see moments for what they were: *incredible gifts worth pursuing all out.*

I promise you that this is not a montage to myself. I think you will see this in a few minutes when I tell you the ways I was falling way short of expectations in these top value areas. I only arrived at these breakthroughs because I recognized that I was nowhere near my potential as a husband, parent and professional. Rather than dwell on it, I got my butt back up and committed to doing something about it. Once I fully connected passion to making moments and defined exactly what that meant in my days, I quickly realized that I had some counterproductive habits that I needed to shift immediately to become a better leader in our household.

Now a shift for all the non-parents out there. If you have people in your life that matter to you, then the opportunity to create powerful transformation still exists here. The most vibrant relationships on the planet are cultivated by individuals who are intentional about investing in them on a consistent daily basis. They only arrive at remarkable because someone steps up to make moments for the people who matter to them most on a consistent basis. Not just when they feel like it. Every single day because that is what it takes to create memories that are remarkable and memorable.

I quickly realized that this concept wasn't just reserved for family and relationships. It turns out that the application was just as powerful for goal-related initiatives. With this new framework in mind, I knew immediately that I wanted to become a world-class moment maker in my career. With *Make Moments* as one of my three lead Motivantras, it radically shifted the way I saw exactly what it is that I did. I was no longer just an author, coach and speaker. I was a person blessed to have gifts that allowed me to create powerful experiences that would drive profound, lasting change in people's lives. If I was disciplined with programming this perspective, I could most definitely create moments that my clients would always remember because it would represent a time that pulled out their highest potential.

This led me to building out content and messages with so much more passion and purpose every single day. It wasn't just a page in a book. It was a meaningful conversation with my reader. With every word I wrote, I started to recognize that I had an opportunity to create a powerful dialogue with people across the world. If I poured into my process and got it right, I could build an experience and relationship with the reader that would last a lifetime. I just needed to create moments that allowed us to go on a journey that was remarkable and memorable. This shift inspired me so much to show up and give more of myself. I decided that masterful moment making was my only option.

I could tell you so many other ways that this *Make Moments* Motivantra radically transformed my life, but that isn't the point here. I only give you these examples because I want you to connect to ways you can apply them to your own life. My passion here lies in helping you realize that you can create mind-blowing shifts in your life by intentionally being more present and purposeful in your top value areas. It's time to be accountable to the value visions you have created for your life. Because you now have outcomes you are passionate about pursuing, it's time to make magical moments in your life.

THINK, BELIEVE AND GO BIGGER

I need to stop right now before moving forward and encourage you to think, believe and go BIGGER. I think we are at a point when I can do this since we now know each other. I have come to realize that this is one of the single most important things I do as a coach when working with people. In a world where you are barraged by the pressure to settle for status quo, I always want to be someone who urges you to strive for extraordinary. Why? I honestly think the better question here is, "Why not?" Why not when you are capable of that? Why not when you have gifts and skill sets lying inside of you just waiting to be used to make remarkable moments in your life? Why not when it will always be possible for you to embrace and EARN extraordinary in your life?

I guess what I am really saying is don't allow yourself to settle for average moments. You are better than that. Don't fall into the trap of settling for mundane. Instead, make flippin moments every single day of your life! Not just ones that keep your life coasting along. Ones that stop you in your tracks and fill you up with an abundance of gratitude and joy. Make the type of moments that add up and allow you to love your life unconditionally. Get in the habit of making ones that momentarily take your breath away so you don't need anything else in your life for it to be complete. Then turn around and make them over and over again so you can string together so many that you create a life that is remarkable and memorable.

Before we get too far ahead of ourselves, I want to make something clear. If I don't, there is a chance that this concept can be used in a way that is overwhelming. I am not meaning that you need to do some grand gesture every single day in each of your value areas. I have seen this same concept play out when encouraging people to practice gratitude in their daily growth routine. It is often challenging at first because people believe that they need a BIG, life altering event to occur to actually complete the exercise. The moment this happens, they have missed the point. Being grateful is not about the next BIG thing. It is about stopping and acknowledging all the incredible gifts you already have around you on a consistent daily basis that most people miss.

The concept of making moments here is exactly the same. A remarkable life begins the moment that a person steps up and commits to bringing their absolute best to the people they love every single day. This is what makes my wife Brandy extraordinary as a parent even when she doesn't know it. It has never been her job to make sure that everything goes perfectly in our household like she sometimes thinks it should. This is flat out not reasonable in any area of life, let alone with kids.

I know what you are probably thinking here. *Not perfect...just passion, Coyte.* If this was your thought, then you are spot on. It has always been to bring love to her role as a parent and she is masterful at that. Remember, sometimes all it takes is an encouraging note from the heart to start stringing together moments.

It is this belief that now drives me on a daily basis. I remind myself every single morning to *Make Moments* in my most important life areas. I just hope

I have done enough here to convince you to do the same. If this resonates with you, simply find one way in your top value area to make that happen today. Commit to show up and make it a must. Once you have done the thing that you believe is making a difference, stop and appreciate your investment. Don't blow past the moment always looking for the next opportunity. Learn to be present enough to be proud that you just took a step to create a life that is worthy of your highest potential.

MY "DON'T ALWAYS GET IT RIGHT" DISCLAIMER

I want to be clear about something. I absolutely don't get this right all the time. Pretty much every single day, there are moments that I miss the mark because I fail to stay present and focused on my most important things. This actually happened a week ago when my son Carter asked me to play cars with him. I didn't feel like it so I told him that I couldn't because I was helping mommy make dinner. The honest truth is that mommy had that locked down and I wanted an excuse to not have to put the ENERGY into running around the house racing with miniature Hot Wheels. It was a missed opportunity and I saw that clearly after the fact. That is why I got it right a couple of minutes later when I remembered what was at stake. I made up for it by going buck wild racing around the living room and kitchen with him.

I have found that the key for me is to remind myself that it is not actually about playing with the cars, dinosaurs or blocks that matters. It is the act of love that matters most. It is a chance to show my kids and wife that they will always be the most important part of my life. It is a chance to prove that they are always worth my time. It is me one act at a time showing them that I love them unconditionally. If I can't give them a 30-minute stretch of my full attention on a consistent basis, then I need to be honest with myself and admit that they are not my top value area. This is something I will never be willing to do so I hold myself accountable to saying "yes" far more often when my most important people need something from me.

Honestly, I have to do the same thing with my work. I tell people all the time that I am passionate about writing books, creating courses and building out keynote talks. Yet if I am not careful, I neglect to give them my time and ENERGY on a consistent daily basis. It seems like this is harder than ever with my dang phone demanding my attention all day long.

Put the dang thing down, Coyte and pour into this book!

The flippin Facebook status update can wait!

Heck, even when I give it my time, I have to remind myself what is at stake. This isn't just writing a chapter. This is stringing together a series of paragraphs that can change the way readers approach living their days. It's an opportunity to radically transform lives if I get it just right. Miss that and I miss the point!

I am no longer willing to miss the point. I have done that plenty in my life and I am over it. If you have neglected being present in the most important areas of your life, I hope you feel the same way here. Here is a little tough love that I often give myself that helps me lock in on my top value areas on a consistent daily basis.

Make no mistake about it, your decisions will eventually compound and turn into something. The question is, "what will that something be?" Will it be something you admire and cherish or something you are disappointed by and wish you could re-do?

I know it sounds dramatic, but this is what is at stake in our lives pretty much every single day.

THE CONSEQUENCES OF BEING INCONSISTENTLY PRESENT

When I reflected on these questions, it caused me to sit down and think about the actual consequences of not consistently being present in the most important areas of my life. I realized that the costs were things like not having a close relationship with my wife and kids. Even more powerful was the fact that I recognized that they would not know how I truly felt about them if I couldn't put my phone down to give them my full attention. In my work, it meant leaving so much of my potential on the table because I would only be giving a half-assed effort. This meant that I would never truly be able to use my gifts to make a difference in the world. I knew that these outcomes would leave me with deep regret down the road.

There was one single question that completely shifted my mindset when considering the impact of my daily decisions.

Am I willing to pay these costs if I keep neglecting top value areas?

The answer was an immediate, resounding NO! I was not willing to fall short in my most important life areas. Not when I could clearly get up each morning and do something about it. I knew better at this point because I had been revisiting my value visions every single morning with emotion. I had trained my brain to know exactly what I was passionate about pursuing and I was no longer willing to pay the costs of being lazy in my approach.

I followed this up by asking another question that was equally powerful.

What outcomes am I willing to fight for?

It didn't take me long to realize that I was willing to fight for the exact visions I had created for my top value areas. I was determined to rise early and make sure I was crystal clear about the father and husband I was passionate about becoming for my family. I would consistently scrap to make this happen no matter what obstacles life threw at me. I also knew that I was willing to fight to create content and experiences that would radically transform my client's lives. In the areas that mattered most, I was game to do whatever it took to make flippin moments that were remarkable and memorable.

The question you need to ask yourself right now is, "Am I willing to show up and fight to make moments in my life?" If the answer is a definite yes, then you are ready to take steps to flip the script on not being present in your life. If not, then we still have some work to do. Or, maybe just mosey on over to the next chapter and hope something sticks there. But before you make any final decision, I would like to introduce you to a concept that just might radically change how you see this entire process.

THE LICENSE TO LIVE YOUR ADVENTURE

In our household, we have a really cool sign above our fireplace that says, *Living Our Adventure*. My sister-in-law Shawna made it for us as a gift when we moved back to Washington state after our tenure decision. It includes the actual maps of all of the states we have lived in since we met. It is such a neat sign because it fits our family perfectly. It's one of the mantras that we try to live by so that we always remember to be intentional about making moments with our kids. It reminds us to take advantage of our surroundings by regularly hiking, taking in sunsets at the beach and climbing mountains together. These things come in abundance in the Pacific Northwest so it only makes sense to capitalize on it.

Why else do I tell you this? Well, because I know that it can be flat out hard to consistently make moments in your life. Showing up every single day to add value to people's lives is challenging. But what if you could shift the way that you see it entirely and make it far more intriguing and inspiring? I bet you would take this opportunity in a second if it was offered to you.

Here's the thing.

This exact thing actually is being offered to you right now.

All you have to do to capitalize is train your brain to see the key areas of your life as an adventure. If you aren't buying it, then just stick with me for a few more minutes.

Every single morning, I use this mantra to urge myself to activate adventure mode in my most important life areas. Of course you know that means having a blast and making moments with my family. But it extends far beyond that. I want my life to be a flippin adventure when it comes to my calling as an author, coach and speaker too. I refuse to fall into the trap of seeing it as an obligation and going through the motions. I want every single book I write from here on out to take readers on a transformational adventure. It is this perspective shift that reminds me to shun the idea of allowing it to become something I "have to" do. Instead, I want to see it as an INCREDIBLE opportunity to create something memorable for readers. I am also passionate about pushing myself way out of my comfort zone so writing the book turns me into a different person in the process.

This was so impactful in my family and work life that I decided to apply it to every single one of my top value areas. Vitality is an area of life that is uber important to me. I know that I need it in abundance to be able to accomplish the BIG dreams I have for my life. I also fully grasp the fact that it is the key to creating a vibrant life. I want to wake up each day and have a wealth of ENERGY that drives me to be extraordinary in the key areas of my life. Rather than see it as an obligation, I choose to see it as an adventure that makes life exciting. This might seem like a small shift, but it has allowed me to see my early morning workouts with my wife in a completely different manner. It's a time when we show up and embark on our fitness journey together. It has also become an adventure that has made our relationship so much stronger and dynamic.

Here is the point:

How you see something matters.

A LOT.

The one thing that I have learned throughout this process is that any part of your life can become an adventure. It's all about perspective. I choose to see my value visions as exciting journeys that will lead me, my family and clients to a remarkable place. You might just think this is semantics, but that isn't accurate. When you learn to see things different than the norm in our society, in a way that pulls out your passion and potential, it radically transforms your life. Is it possible for me to see family, work and vitality as an obligation? You bet your ass I could! This would put me right into a pile with the millions of people who fall short of their New Year's resolutions each year. The moment you see your desired outcomes as an unappealing outcome you "have to" pursue, you have already lost the battle.

There is an incredible hack that you can access here to create powerful change in your life. Teach your brain to see your top value visions as a MASSIVE opportunity. You already know this though so let's take it to an entirely different level. Learn to see them as an adventure or an escapade. Just using these words changes things entirely because your brain sees them as pleasurable and is far more likely to pursue your desired outcomes as a result. This is exactly why I choose to remind myself to *live my adventure* every single morning when revisiting my value visions. I want to associate all kinds of pleasure with going all in to pursue my dreams.

If you don't believe me, then just give it a try sometime in one of your most important life areas. It's often good to do it with something that you are dreading in these areas. Rather than sit back and dwell on the situation, release the "have to" mentality that we previously discussed and look for the reason you are "blessed to" be able to do it. Flood your brain with that opportunity. Even if it is one single thing that you can capitalize on, point your brain to that and remind yourself that you get a chance to do something unique.

The lesson here is that your life will be much more rewarding if you stack the deck in your favor to experience happiness. Focusing on what you don't like in your situation will never get you emotions that enhance your quality of life. There is no question that there will be times when you need to eliminate people and initiatives from your environment. If that's not possible in the short-term, point your brain to a productive point that allows you to make your life vibrant. Rather than seeing obligation, consistently remind it to find adventure and allow yourself to be blown away by how this type of programming will radically elevate your quality of life.

THE MAGNITUDE OF MOMENT MAKING

When you think about it, making moments really is a big deal. It is the essence of what makes life special. You can have all the money in the world and it won't matter if you don't take the time to make special memories with the people you love most. None of the actual material accomplishments that you have garnered will likely matter at the end of your life, but the things you did to create magical moments with your kids, friends, spouse, clients and family members will. The most inspiring thing to remind yourself is that this is something that is always within your control if you become present in your approach to living.

I am going to encourage you consistently in these final pages to flat out make moments that are remarkable and memorable in your life. But I also want to be completely honest about what it's going to take to make this happen. I don't want to be one of those self-help gurus promising instant, incredible breakthroughs by simply focusing on them. I want to be completely straight with you. So, here it goes.

You've got to take real action in your life to get remarkable and memorable.

It will flat out NEVER happen if you don't learn to be fully present in the most important moments in your life.

Instead, you need to lock in on your "Sacred Space" periods in your day and give them your full time, ENERGY and focus. You've got to do this even when you don't feel like it.

It isn't easy to become a person who consistently makes moments. The truth is that there are consistently going to be times when your kids are acting like wild, rabid animals and they make you question whether anything you are doing as a parent is working at all. There are also going to be instances when your motivation and ENERGY levels wane so much that you don't feel like following through on your intentions at all. And there will be occasions when you fall short of expectations and that will be so disappointing that you won't want to take even one more step forward.

I am here to tell you that it is in these moments that you will carve out your path to a remarkable and memorable life.

Anybody can do it when it's easy. It's the individuals who lock down and follow through even when they don't feel like it that eventually EARN extraordinary in their top value areas. The key is to fend off the urge to be lazy and instead commit to fighting to be fully present in the most important times in your day. I guess what I am really trying to say is that you are capable of a flippin incredible life, but only if you learn to embrace the incredible moments that are currently present in your life. Once you get this right, you will be ready to bring the best you have to offer to the people that matter to you most and that will be more than enough.

FLIPPIN NOT PRESENT

It's so flippin easy to get caught up in the crazy clutter of living. While this can seem harmless, the truth is that we are being robbed of something truly special every single day when we fail to be fully present in our lives. Without realizing it, we give away the opportunity to make moments that are truly remarkable and memorable with the people and things that matter to us most. I hope you can see that this is a cost that you should never be willing to pay. Failing to be present enough to give our top value areas our full time, ENERGY and focus will only lead us to disappointment. This is exactly why it is the perfect time to flip the script on not present once and for all. It is time to step up and make moments that allow you to create a life that you will always be proud of.

YELLOW BALL #8

THE "WHAT IF YOU HAD ONE WEEK?" HABIT

What if you had one week left in your life? How would you live if you knew that your time on this planet was limited? If you are anything like me, I bet you would see your life completely different. Rather than taking your most important people for granted, I am guessing that you would stop and look at them with reverence. You would likely find unique things in them that you hadn't seen in quite a while. If you have kids, I am willing to bet that their acting up wouldn't bother you quite as much anymore. Instead, you would just embrace the moments with them and see the time as an incredible opportunity to love them with all your heart regardless of their behavior. Normal everyday things that you experience would be completely different. You would likely find beauty in your environment that you had been missing in the clutter of living.

When I was challenged to do this activity, I was almost finished with this book. It initially made me feel good to know I was spending most of my time on the things that mattered to me most. That is what this flip the script process had done for me. But I also realized that I still wasn't quite living at a level that would satisfy me if I had limited time in my life. I knew I wanted to love my family a lot more. I thought about how much more goofy I would be so we could laugh like crazy every single day. I immediately knew I wanted to look at my wife with more passion and reverence every single day. I realized I wanted to step up and find an entirely different level urging people to live with more vibrancy in their lives. I wanted to be more present so I could make more moments that were remarkable and memorable.

Here's the thing I reminded myself and want to make clear to you. You don't have to wait to live like this. You can experience this urgency to live with passion and purpose right now at this exact moment. Don't wait until you are short of time to live a life you are truly passionate about. Take action right away so you can use it up every single day and be proud of the moments that you are making. That is your activity for this chapter. Keep it simple. Just identify one way you could consistently make moments in your top value area and act on it right away today. Then rinse and repeat this exercise with your other top value areas over the next week. Make this approach your norm and you will quickly become a moment maker like my wife Brandy!

"

A REMARKABLE LIFE BEGINS

THE MOMENT THAT A PERSON
STEPS UP AND COMMITS TO

BRINGING THEIR
ABSOLUTE BEST

TO THE PEOPLE THEY LOVE MOST
EVERY SINGLE DAY

CHAPTER 9

FL!PING

GOOD, BUT NOT GREAT

BRING THE BLISS...LIKE A BOSS

*"The soul should always stand ajar, ready to welcome
the ecstatic experience."*
—Emily Dickinson

I was sitting in a beautiful ballroom at the Marriott in Santa Clara, California. For the last four days, Brandy and I had enjoyed learning about building a thriving business at Experts Academy with Brendon Burchard. It was the final day and Brendon was talking about the steps necessary to succeed when you leave the event and are on your own. He arrived at a point when he got very serious before asking the audience, "Do you want to know the single one thing that has made the biggest difference in my career? This is the one thing that has driven my career more than anything else." This immediately caught my attention as I locked in waiting for his response. After a few suspenseful, quiet seconds, he proclaimed, "A reverence for living. I have learned to absolutely love what I do and that drives me on a daily basis."

I have no idea if this thought hit the other attendees as hard as it hit me. It was by far the most powerful lesson that I learned the entire weekend. It made me realize that this is what it was going to take to be truly unique in my top value areas. It was never going to be enough to simply show up and go through the motions. To create moments that were remarkable and memorable, I was going to have to find a way to bring more ENERGY, passion and love to my life. This thought inspired me because I knew that this was something I could always control. I couldn't control all of the outcomes I was after, but I could control my own process and how I lived the moments in my days.

Brendon went on to explain how this reverence for living has radically impacted his career and life. Of course there were times when he didn't feel like doing something. But he also explained that it was in these moments that he urged himself to have a deep respect for living. It made me realize that reverence for living was one of his Motivantras that had driven him to live at a higher level in his value areas. It was this focal point that drove him to show up and bring bliss to his calling. I had just witnessed this in person as Brendon had brought incredible joy for four days straight at the event despite having pneumonia right before it. I knew my next step.

It was time to find my own focal point that would allow me to cultivate a real reverence for living in the key areas of my life.

FROM GOOD TO GREAT...

It was a gorgeous Spring afternoon in the Pacific Northwest so I decided to take a hike on one of my all-time favorite trails in Anacortes. We were blessed that the house we were renting backed up to over 20 miles of picturesque nature trails. I put on my hiking shoes and made my way towards Whistle Lake. The breathtaking views immediately flooded my senses and put me into a completely relaxed state. I started to reflect on the idea of reverence for living. This is when an intriguing insight hit me.

My life is going pretty dang good. I've got a lot of solid things going on right now.

This was definitely a welcoming series of thoughts because of the challenging spot I had been in just three years earlier. I had struggled to get my bearings after my tenure decision and I was finally regaining some real order in my life.

I was consistently landing keynote talks around the country.

I was attracting proactive coaching clients.

I was making moments with my most important people.

I was starting to attract enough business to support my family.

Honestly, it was a nice feeling to know that things were starting to fall into place. While the chaos of losing my job had taught me invaluable lessons, I have to admit that I welcomed normalcy and the good things that were starting to happen around me. I felt like we deserved it after all the challenges we had faced and conquered the past few years. I was definitely proud of my family's progress.

This is when I also realized that I had arrived at a critical juncture in my journey. With some of our goals starting to fall into place, it would be easy to draw back and settle for comfortable. I knew from experience that this is exactly when complacency can kick in. It's the subtle space where you start to settle for average without even knowing it.

There is actually some science that shows why this trend is so common in human beings. In studying the brain while writing this book, I stumbled upon a fascinating concept about how our mind makes daily decisions. When left on its own, our brain will generally choose the option that maximizes ENERGY in the moment. It actually turns out that this often tends to be the path of least resistance. This evolved as a necessary survival mechanism when human beings were less modern and didn't know where their next meal was coming from. It made sense to make decisions that preserved ENERGY.

But there's a problem with that model. Most of us no longer have these same threats in our surrounding environment. In fact, if you are reading this book, it's likely that you have a wide range of adequate food and shelter options that meet all your basic needs. Yet even with these amenities, we still have the same outdated software system in our brain and will often subconsciously choose the path of least resistance to conserve ENERGY. The problem is that this often leads us to making less than ideal daily decisions that rob us of our ability to live to our highest potential. That is, unless we use our conscious brain to override this programming and give our brain a much better option.

Now back to my situation. I was now doing pretty dang good. It would be easy to stay at this level and settle for comfortable. But I had reflected and knew what was at stake.

I'm not willing to settle for good in my most important value areas.

Not when I'm capable of great.

Not when I have so much more untapped potential inside me!

It was time to give my brain a much better option. If I was going to flip the script on good enough once and for all, I had to give my mind a much better focal point than just average. I sensed that I had been put on this planet for a reason and it was time to find out exactly what that meant. This is when the previous flips I had made in my journey started to really pay dividends.

Not easy...EARN IT!

Not fit in...STAND OUT!

It was this desire to be different that drove me to seek out an entirely different level in my approach to living. I wanted to know with certainty that I was showing up each day and bringing my absolute best to my top value areas.

I wanted to use it up!

I wanted my life to be vibrant!

I wanted to have a flippin reverence for living!

I wasn't quite there yet, but I knew it was possible. After all, I had witnessed it first hand from a mentor that I admired. Now I just needed to figure out how to make a reverence for living my new norm.

PURSUE PASSION PART II

We have already emphasized the importance of actively pursuing passion in this book. I thought it made sense to bring it back here for a sequel because it's one of the core foundations for tapping into higher-level emotional states. I have to admit that I had it all wrong during the early part of my journey when it came to passion. I would sit around expecting it to come to me. Then I started to realize that there was a wonderful trend that emerged on the days when I tapped into emotion during my morning growth routine.

When I drum up emotion in my core habits, I find myself more and more passionate about pursuing my top value areas in my life.

This naturally drove new intentional action that built momentum and led my inspiration to an all-time high. This is when another transformative insight hit me.

Passion is all about the pursuit. When I intentionally pursue it in my daily routine, it becomes omnipresent and drives my actions in a powerful manner.

Once I knew this, I had no choice but to get up and pursue passion every single morning. Low and behold, it continued to escalate in my life. In the rare moments when I stumbled and focused on what my life was not, my passion would wane and I would struggle in my approach. This is when I would focus on flipping the script by pointing my brain to the baseline blessings in my life. As I emphasized feeling a deep sense of gratitude for them, my passion would start to become omnipresent again and my meaningful actions would come more consistently and effortlessly. I was starting to learn to tap into the power of intentional emotional states.

The biggest shifts I experienced initially when emphasizing *Pursue Passion* came in my work. It was a natural extension from what I learned from Brendon Burchard. As I placed a priority on passion in my most important priorities, it allowed me to finally understand what it meant to love my work unconditionally. It was as if all of my shifts were coming together and allowing me to see my calling as an incredible blessing. This didn't happen by accident. It only started to occur because I trained my brain to focus on possible. Once my perspective changed, I began to cultivate a reverence for my life.

The end outcome was experiencing "Sacred Space" time periods each day when I felt an incredible sense of gratitude for the opportunity to create and deliver transformational experiences. I started to absolutely love what I was doing. Not surprisingly, these higher vibrancy states allowed me to experience new creativity that led to fresh innovations in my coaching sessions, keynote talks and writing this book. It made me realize even more that our focus is the key to transformation in our lives. I now knew that this was something I could always control.

I tell you these things because this was not the norm five years earlier. When I was at the University of North Carolina, I definitely liked my work, but I was not focusing on things that allowed me to consistently be crazy passionate about it. I was too caught up in doing things for the wrong reasons. I was so concerned about getting approval and attention that I forgot why I had even become a professor in the first place. I had missed the point. I was not intentionally living with a perspective that would bring real passion to my daily approach. But that was then and this was now. I had learned a valuable lesson that was about to help me experience one of the ultimate spices of life.

THE ULTIMATE SPICE OF LIFE

The song *Happier* by Marshmello and Bastille was blasting away on my Bose noise-cancelling headphones. I was dancing wildly through my downstairs area as I felt a surge of ENERGY shoot throughout my entire body.

I want to do everything in my power to help my family and clients be happy every single day in their life. It's totally possible and they deserve that!

As I transitioned into my office and settled in front of one of my favorite quote graphics, I felt a calm come over my entire body.

It's totally possible to be happy at any moment if you just get really good at focusing on the right things.

It was a thought that came to me with crystal clarity. I immediately got goosebumps all over my body. Whenever I arrive at this physiological response, I have learned that I have stumbled on a powerful insight that deserves my full attention.

As I sat at my desk digesting what I had just experienced in my quirky movement + music routine, I realized I had just stumbled upon one of the coolest lessons I had learned in my entire flip the script journey. Heck, it was one of the coolest lessons I have ever absorbed in my entire life. Do you want to hear exactly what it was?

It's possible to control emotions.

Ok, I admit that this probably doesn't seem all that profound given that we have loosely touched on it at various points throughout the book. Let me give it another run.

It's possible to drum up ANY emotion at ANY moment with the right perspective and programming!

That one sounds a lot more intriguing, doesn't it? Now that I have your attention, let's delve into this one a little deeper.

Who wouldn't want to be able to immediately get themselves into a blissful state in an instant if given the option? I think it is safe to say that no reasonable person would deny this capability. It seems to me that this would be the ultimate super human capacity. Want to be happy? Boom! Just like that, put your cape on and you are happy as all get out! All right, so there might not be a cape, but I do believe that there is an approach that makes it possible to experience this exact desirable emotion in an instant. It seems completely unreasonable, right? I think I would have thought the same thing at one point too because my brain and body were littered with disappointment, frustration and overwhelm.

Is it possible to replicate these emotions of joy and complete calm that I experienced in my morning routine?

I wasn't quite sure, but I determined that I would find out by showing up and striving each day to pull out passion with my music + movement ritual. It didn't take me long to realize that my emotions were replicable in this environment. Not only that, but I started to get even better at identifying movements, focal points and strategies to take my emotions to an entirely different level. It was at this point that I knew that it was possible to get myself into a higher-level emotional state in an instant.

Given this was the case, I assumed that I could accomplish the same thing in my "Sacred Space" time frames in my day. The actual emotional outcomes I desired might be slightly different, but the pursuit was the same. I determined that I wanted to start to create from a space of unconditional love when working on this book. I wanted to *Give and Grow* at a crazy high level. With some trial and error, I eventually recognized a simple process that allowed me to reach a creative peak consistently. As I sat down to write each day, I would hop up and down for a few seconds (inspiration from my competitive wrestling days), clap my hands three times and remind myself to *Speak Life* before I begin a chapter. This would put me into a creative state where adding value was my central focus.

In my family life, I would set the tone in my morning routine and at sporadic times during my day. In honor of my music + movement habit, I started to listen to songs intentionally that triggered passion in my most important relationships in my life. *A Million Dreams* on The Greatest Showman soundtrack made me think about climbing 10,000 plus foot mountains with my son Carter. *Girl On Fire* by Alicia Keys made me think about my spunky little girl Mya CRUSHING IT in her life in the future. *Turn the Lights Down Low* by DJ Max Turn made me think about Brandy and…yea-a-a-a-h, this really isn't that type of book, but you get the point. These songs triggered passion and put me into an inspired state that made me want to show up and make moments with my tribe.

When I combined all of these experiences, I realized that I had arrived at a pretty special realization about life. So often, we constantly seek out outcomes in our environment that will ultimately bring us happiness and other desirable emotions. Yet they seem to avoid us as we pursue external outcomes, praise and status.

All along, the emotions we so desperately want to experience are inside of us. The truth is that we can access them at any moment by controlling our focus and programming our brain to intentionally pursue productive pleasure. That is what these powerful experiences taught me.

The ability to experience high-level emotions is the spice of life and it is something that you have the power to access with the right approach.

The final thing I want to point out here is the outcome that occurred when I was intentional about pursuing optimal emotional states. I started to notice that my brain started to naturally gravitate towards these desirable outcomes during my days. That is when it hit me.

I had trained my brain and cells in my body to become addicted to these emotions.

As a result, it had become their norm and they were seeking out ways to experience them on their own. I knew this was possible because I had recently read how our brain and cells get addicted to negative states like chaos, disappointment, frustration and sadness. I had flipped the script on undesirable emotions by training my brain to expect the opposite!

For me, one of the triggers for this radical shift was listening to Brendon Burchard talk about a reverence for living that fall day in Santa Clara. It provided a seed thought for refusing to settle for anything less than extraordinary emotions. Rather than wait around for fleeting moments when he loved his life, he instead got out and made reverence his ritual and standard. As a thought leader, he refused to believe the status quo and instead set his own standard for excellence and living. This example inspired me to get out and find my own way to love my life unconditionally. *No more settling for mundane emotions! I am committed to accessing high level states that make my life truly vibrant!* It was right around this time that I took another step forward and found an entirely different level of living.

BRING THE BLISS

There are shifts in life that put into motion a change that increases your life a decent amount. *Not bad.* Then there are ones that are so profound that they completely catch you off guard and blow the lid off of your potential. *Whoa, didn't see that one coming!* The shift I am about to break down fits this second description to a "T". I had gotten to the point where I was really doing pretty good with all of the flips I had made in my life. Things were trending upward and I had new opportunities that I was excited about. However, truth be told, I was still nowhere near my highest potential. My recent encounters with tapping into high emotional states made me realize I was on to something special.

I knew I needed a new focal point to help me access my optimal states on a consistent daily basis. I was brainstorming one day when the word bliss kept popping up in my reading. Eventually I started to think there was something to it so I wrote it down and made it an emphasis in my morning routine. It didn't take long for it to dawn on me that this was the ideal state to start pursuing on a consistent daily basis. I immediately started to look for a Motivantra that would drive my pursuit in this area. *BRING the BLISS! Yes, that's it!* I was so pleased with my new invention that I immediately went upstairs to tell Brandy about it. This quickly became the name for one of the coolest habits in our household.

As we began to work on building a family culture, my wife started to talk about how it would be cool to dance as a family once a day. She explained that it would be neat to get out of our comfort zone and teach our kids some valuable lessons. Brandy also had the brilliant idea of calling the new habit "BRING the BLISS." Every evening when it was time to rock it out, we didn't say, "Hey, let's go dance." We would excitedly announce, "Time to BRING the BLISS!" Honestly, this seems like a small shift, but it made a world of difference because it became easier to sell it to our kids.

Our son Carter, who was seven at the time, initially refused to do the activity entirely. I am not necessarily surprised because being at school had started to build up a desire to tone it down and fit in. We knew what was at stake here so we didn't back off one bit. Instead, we went about our business getting buck wild dancing and BRINGING the BLISS. It didn't take long until it looked so fun that he decided to join us. I have to admit that it's a good thing because he is hands down the most creative dancer in our household. Our little man can moonwalk, disco and shake his booty like a champ. It brings us so much joy to see him cut loose and do his thing!

Just for a moment, I want you to imagine the four of us dancing in our living room to the *Trolls* and *Madagascar 3* soundtracks. All of a sudden, I get the urge to clear out the ottoman so our kids can do a solo. As Brandy and I clap our hands and drum up atmosphere, our daughter Mya jumps in the middle and starts dancing wildly with a monster grin on her face. I pause for a moment and feel an overwhelming sense of gratitude for what is occurring. My beautiful daughter is experiencing an abundance of joy and happiness. What I am seeing on her face is pure bliss.

Brandy and I have learned that there is so much more than fun at stake in these moments. It isn't just a little quirky dancing (which would be more than enough by the way!). It's an opportunity to show our kids the importance of choosing incredible emotional states in life's "littler" moments. It is a chance to show them how to take something that could be mundane and morph it into something magical. It's an unexpected yellow ball habit that allows them to learn how to perform a flippin Houdini act on their emotions every single day of their lives. It's also a way for us to urge our kids to always know that *Not Fit In...STAND OUT* is the normal standard operating procedure in our household.

There is nothing normal about bringing bliss to standard every day activities. *But THAT is exactly the point!* We aren't here still investing late in this book to mail it in. You would have quit eight chapters ago if mundane was your maxim. Now that we have started to stack some serious habits, our job now is to flip the idea of "good enough" and challenge you to stretch your capacity. Honestly, I want to push enough here to help you blow the lid off of your potential. I believe it in my core that the way to do this is by pursuing optimal emotional states. It's time to flip the script on average emotions and make bliss, happiness, joy or any other state you desire in life your norm.

All I really want to accomplish in this chapter is to help you bring some serious passion into your life. Rather than walking around feeling disappointed or decent, why not step up and remind yourself to BRING the BLISS to your top value areas? While it will be challenging at first, I think you will be blown away by how a simple Motivantra can radically shift your mindset and emotions if you are consistent at programming and pursuing it. In the middle of this process you have the power to learn how to ratchet up your emotions in an instant when you grab hold of your focus. This is the exact moment your life will change in ways you never previously imagined possible.

Honestly, the coolest shift in my work came when I stopped worrying so much about outcomes outside of my control and instead urged myself to just BRING the BLISS. I didn't need to be perfect. I just needed to bring passion, ENERGY and love to my most important work initiatives. This single programming emphasis breathed new life into this book, my new ETR coaching programs and my keynote talks. Each time I sat down to create, I reminded myself to BRING the BLISS whether I felt like it or not. Eventually I got enough repetitions in that my brain got on board and it started to become my norm to pursue passion when moving into my "Sacred Space" time frames.

I realized that I had something truly special here the first time I brought this concept up to my coaching club. I didn't think much about it at the time, but I started to talk to them about the BRING the BLISS philosophy. Shortly afterwards, I started to get emails and messages from members thanking me for being blissful in my approach. Then they kept telling me about how they were BRINGING the BLISS with their families and loved ones. One older guy actually said that he and his wife had started to BRING the BLISS every single morning together and it was a blast. No, he was not talking about sex (although this can certainly become a perk when this becomes a top Motivantra for both partners!) He was talking about the wild dancing they did together to start their days as a couple. It made me smile to hear this and immediately inspired me to dedicate an entire chapter to the concept in this book.

...LIKE A BOSS

I didn't just want to BRING the BLISS just occasionally when I felt like it. I knew I was passionate about making it my normal standard of living in every single part of my life. With this being the case, I started to challenge myself to take bringing bliss to an entirely different level. I didn't want marginal ENERGY. I wanted to bring it full force every single day.

I wanted to bring it like a...Beast? *Well, that could work.*

Or, how about a...Badass? *It worked for Jen Sincero so maybe it would work for me too.*

Let's try one more. How about like a...Boss? *Yeah, I like that one!*

It spoke to me so I started to encourage myself to bring my bliss making to an entirely different level. Here's the thing though. You need to choose a focal point that fits you or it flat out won't work. In the words of Marie Kondo, pick whatever one sparks joy for you and then use it to tidy up your life.

I can't just tell you to BRING the BLISS like a boss and then move on.

This requires a little more explanation. What does this even mean? It means far more than shunning the status quo in your life. I think it means actually stepping up and finally fully owning extraordinary in the key areas of your life. Rather than sitting around hoping for the right emotions to spark action, this quirky Motivantra is custom designed to inspire you to get out and make bliss, passion and vibrancy an absolute MUST in your life. Why not when you flippin can, right? It's time to start owning your ability to have far better than "pretty decent" in your life. It's time to BRING THE BLISS...LIKE A FLIPPIN BOSS!

I started to realize that this Motivantra was my kryptonite to coasting and settling in my life. In the moments when I didn't feel like it, I would call up the value visions in my life and remind myself WHY I was willing to fight for them. I would do whatever was necessary to drum up an electric emotional response to them. It turned out to be really effective to use these focal points to interrupt my lazy patterns.

Don't feel like dancing with the kids? *Too bad my man! Pony up and BRING the BLISS anyways! If you want to be a dad that your kids will admire, then you need to step up and give them a reason to!*

Don't want to go to a meeting? *It doesn't matter! You chose this and it is your job to still bring your A game! Step up and make some moments!*

The point is that you need to stop in these moments and be intentional about choosing your response. Bliss and any other higher level emotion only become possible when you purposefully point your brain to opportunity consistently.

It may take you a little while to grasp this concept, but don't let off the gas pedal. The first step will be simply reminding yourself to bring bliss, joy or any other desirable emotional state to your most important value areas. Do that consistently enough and eventually your brain will simply know that this is the expectation at set times during your day. You will eventually establish a new baseline of passion in your normal daily interactions. It's at this point that you will have a unique opportunity to take things to an uncommon level. Why? Because once BRING the BLISS becomes your norm, you will have an incredible chance to inspire others to experience what it is like to live with joy and vibrancy on a daily basis.

THE CAPACITY TO CRUSH IT...

It's totally true. You have the capacity to CRUSH IT in the key areas of your life. You can live at a level consistently that makes your life remarkable and memorable. I know that because you are still here with me fighting for it and striving to do your thing. I can just imagine you intentionally showing up in your top values each day ready to give the absolute best you have to offer. It fires me up just thinking about this! No matter what life throws you, remind yourself that this is always possible. You can ALWAYS bring your best attitude, effort and focus to the areas of life that matter to you most.

Here's the honest truth though.

You won't ever live to your highest potential settling for mundane emotions.

Once you start to truly grasp the "flip the script" concept, there is no room for habitual states like anger, disappointment, frustration and overwhelm. Not when you are capable of consistently choosing emotions that make your life vibrant and dynamic. It might seem like a stretch now, but you will inevitably close the gap mentally if you are simply willing to try out habits that give your brain better, more empowering options.

You already know that it's easy to start taking your top values for granted. Refuse to allow this to happen. Every single day, there will be distractions knocking at your door ready to take your focus away from the things that matter the most. Cut through the clutter by stepping up and reminding yourself of the person you are passionate about becoming in your life. As this starts to excite you, get a little wild in your approach by encouraging yourself to BRING the

BLISS in your "Sacred Space" time periods. Don't be afraid to get a little funky so you can learn what it's like to be able to flip the script on average emotions.

FLIPPIN MUNDANE EMOTIONS

Nobody dreamed as a kid of feeling just all right when they grew up. Most of us visualized ourselves accomplishing really cool things so we could experience the joy that accompanies these rewarding outcomes. The point is that we never actually desired flippin mundane emotions that would give us an average existence. Why would you then or right now? There is no reason to ever settle for average in your life. When people ask you how you are doing, I want you to be able to answer, "Flippin remarkable! Why, thank you for asking!" All right, so you don't have to rub it in or use my terminology, but you get the point. It's entirely possible for you to drum up emotions that make your life so vibrant that you love it unconditionally. It's time to refuse to accept any habitual emotions that don't fit the life you would love to be living. Instead, let's flip the script on mundane emotions so you can make each day an incredible adventure.

YELLOW BALL #9
THE "BRING THE BLISS" HABIT

I thought about giving you a couple options here, but I just can't do it. There is only one activity here that taught me to tap into my highest emotional states. It was a game changer for me so I want to urge you to give it a run. Grab your headphones and find a song on your phone that gets you all fired up. Try to pick one that gives you an emotional response that inspires you.

Once you have this ready, go to a space where you are comfortable cutting loose and challenge yourself to do your thing. Just crank up the music and BRING the BLISS like a boss my friend! Clap your hands, wave your arms above your head and/or dance wildly around the room. If it feels a little to funky at first, just jump up and down until a better option presents itself. As you do this, allow the music and motion to drum up your brain's ability to visualize the really cool things that you want to attract into your life.

The ultimate goal here is to tap into a full on "passion pulsing through your veins" moment. If you really get it right, you will get goosebumps all over your body because you are so excited about where your life is going in the future. If this doesn't work, then try different music and movement options until you connect with an emotional reaction that sparks vision. Then just keep finding new ways to BRING the BLISS for 66-days until you are consistently experiencing all the emotions you desire.

"

ONCE YOU MAKE

BRINGING THE BLISS YOUR NORM,

YOU WILL HAVE AN INCREDIBLE OPPORTUNITY TO
INSPIRE OTHERS TO EXPERIENCE WHAT IT IS LIKE TO

LIVE WITH
JOY & VIBRANCY

ON A DAILY BASIS
THE WORLD NEEDS MORE OF THAT

CHAPTER 10

FL!P

ING

◆— SELF-DEFEATING CHATTER —◆

SPEAK LIFE...
INTO YOUR OWN LIFE

"It's not what you say out of your mouth that determines your life.
It's what you whisper to yourself that has the most power."
—**Robert Kiyosaki**

I was sitting at practice one day when my coach Ron walked up and said to me, "I think you should go to the Cadet World Team Trials. It is the first year they are allowing 14-year olds to go and I think it would be really good for you." After some discussion, I agreed that it would be a solid experience. There was just one catch. Because the tournament was geared for 15 and 16-year olds, I would have to get a note from my doctor saying it would be all right for me to compete. I was a little skeptical of this, but Ron was my guy so I went home to ask my parents if I could go. They quickly said yes and I was off to the doctor's office to get a letter clearing me for competition. I wasn't sure if I was ready, but I was off to Chicago, Illinois for my first major national tournament.

Once I arrived at Welsh-Ryan Arena on the campus of Northwestern University, I started to size up my competition. I was naturally pretty competitive so I knew all of the top kids who would likely be at the tournament. I was well aware of the fact that Steven Bradley from Indiana was the #1 kid in the country. I also knew that David Stoltz was a veteran from Illinois who was currently the #2 ranked kid in the United States. I was pretty much dialed in on every single wrestler in the Top 10. The reason I knew this was because I had it in my head that I wanted to be at the top of the list within the next couple years.

Early in the tournament, I strolled up to the bracket to see who I would have for my next match. As I glanced at my placement, I paused for a moment as doubt creeped into my mind.

I have Steven Bradley, the #1 kid in the country.

Here's the thing. On top of being the top ranked wrestler in the United States, I had seen Bradley wrestle already and he was bald, jacked and looked like he could have eaten me if he wanted to. *Ok, I am exaggerating for effect here, but he was scary looking.* As you can imagine, reminding yourself that you have the #1 wrestler in the country with this type of mindset is not productive when going into a match. It flat out isn't conducive to winning.

I was walking away from the bracket when I glanced up to see my coach Ron walking towards me. In his normal casual manner, he had a big old grin on his face and his eyes were all lit up like a kid on Christmas. I learned over time that he was always like this when we were at big tournaments. While other coaches were all grim and serious, he had a way of carrying himself that made you relax and look forward to competition.

"What's up buddy?" asked Ron. "You ready to wrestle?"

I shrugged my shoulders and responded, "Yeah, I guess so."

"What do you mean, you guess so?" replied Ron with only a minor concern on his face. "Well, what's up?"

I hesitated for a moment and contemplated what to say. After a few seconds, I blurted out, "I have Steven Bradley…the #1 kid in the country."

Ron's smile widened across his face as he looked straight into my eyes.

"No, he has you. The #1 kid in the country has to deal with you. He has the bad draw."

I have to admit that his response caught me completely off guard. My immediate thought was, *but has he seen Steven Bradley? The guy is a grown man.* But as I reflected, I realized that Ron had not flinched one bit when he had said that to me. I knew he was completely genuine in his belief that I was the bad draw. He patted me on the back and walked away as I got into my warm-up.

As I started to jog and roll out my shoulders, I thought to myself, *Could Ron be right? Is it true that Steven Bradley has to deal with me?*

At first, I shot it down, thinking that this couldn't be right since he was the top guy in the country and I was just a 14-year old kid. But I kept coming back to what Ron had said, wondering if it was true. I had to at least consider it because he had invested in me so much. Ron cared about me in a way that no other coach or leader had ever cared about me before. It was because of this that I eventually started to believe that it might be true.

It was incredible. Within a 20-minute period, I had went from believing that *I had the #1 kid in the country* to *the #1 kid in the country has to deal with me.* I am convinced that Ron's belief in me single handedly made the difference in how I approached this tournament.

I felt so confident when I stepped out on the mat that day. I immediately got into my offense and never once let off the gas pedal during the match. It didn't matter at all that I was only 14-years old. Nor did it make any difference that I wasn't even ranked. What mattered is that I truly believed that I belonged out there.

I defeated the #1 kid in the country in the match and went on to defeat #2 David Stoltz from Illinois in the finals. I became the first ever 14-year old to make the Cadet World Team. But it wasn't the outcome that truly mattered.

In a moment when I questioned myself, Ron stepped into my life and taught me to believe in my abilities. As a 14-year old kid at my first national tournament, I was not completely sure if I belonged there or not. I am pretty sure I was thinking that it was a great opportunity to compete hard and get experience. I honestly wasn't sure if I was enough to compete with the top guys in the country. Then Ron stepped into my life and shifted my entire mindset in an instant. It was in this moment that he taught me the incredible power available to elevate your performance in an instant when you believe you are capable.

THE FLIP SIDE OF A "FULL BELIEF" FOCUS

I wish I could say that I carried this powerful lesson with me in my back pocket for the rest of my life. And each time I needed it, I simply pulled it out and reminded myself that I was more than enough. I didn't, but you already know that. Life can be funny because sometimes we have already learned all the lessons we need to excel, but we get caught up in the clutter of living and forget about them. In the process, we also tend to pick up other negative habits that create a drag on our potential. In my instance, I learned some limiting belief systems that allowed me to experience the flip side of the "full belief" focus I had learned with Ron.

These were front and center in the weeks and months following my UNC tenure decision. When I officially lost my job, a variety of barriers popped up in front of me in the form of negative noise, focusing on not enough and an instant gratification mindset. One-by-one, I had found ways to flip the script on these so I could close the gap on my goals. Then I ran into a new opponent in the form of self-defeating inner chatter that kept popping up and trying to talk me down from pursuing my dream. I knew immediately that this pattern was causing me to draw back in my approach. Once I saw this clearly, I knew it was time to flip the script on this self-defeating inner chatter.

I was reading *The Untethered Soul* one morning by Michael Singer when he introduced the idea of a negative "inner roommate" that is living inside our brains. It fascinated me to hear him say that this voice is often completely neurotic as it will jump from one side of an opinion to another in a matter of seconds. Rather than allow this to continue, Singer explained that it's important to first simply notice the dialogue and remind yourself that it's not you. It's the "inner roommate" that he previously referred to. Once you have paid attention to what this person has to say over an extended period of time, you will realize that it's an incredibly negative roomie that is ruining parts of your life. This is when you will know that it is time to get rid of this voice because it's not serving you one bit.

Once I started to apply the concepts outlined by Singer, I was blown away by how much inner dialogue I still had running below the surface. I had already done so much work to redirect my brain, but there was still another world of chatter that I had not fully been aware of. I think this is probably true for most people. We notice some moments of negative self-talk, but we don't realize that we actually have an inner voice that likes to run pretty much non-stop around the clock. The problem is that this "inner roommate" is often one that is criticizing us and telling us why we aren't enough. Its intentions might be in the right place, but it's totally hurting our ability to achieve really cool things in our lives.

As I started to track this, I immediately realized that I had some work to do to breakthrough in my career and life. My inner voice was still there silently urging me to back off of aspirations.

What if you fall short?

What if the whole UNC thing happens again?

You should probably just cool it and play it safe for now.

The fascinating thing is that I really had no idea that this voice was still playing these types of messages. This inner dialogue had been going on for so long that I had stopped even noticing it. When it wasn't focused on why I should draw back on my aspirations, it was often spouting nonsense that lowered my quality of living. *No, there is nobody waiting in the downstairs closet to get me!*

An incredible thing happened once I began to notice this inner chatter. I started to see this "inner chatter" as something that was a choice. I no longer just thought it was something that was just a part of me. Instead, I took Singer's advice and started to see my voices as a bad roommate that had overstayed his welcome. Never in a million years would I allow someone to stick around and talk to me in this manner. Even when it wasn't negative, this roommate was all over the place with his opinion. It was just too much to put up with anymore. So I decided that it was time to do something about this needy, negative roommate.

SHUT YOUR MOUTH...AND GET OUT!!!

I decided that the best option was to confront this roommate that had overstayed his welcome. I knew I needed to make a statement so I could create immediate space in my brain to redirect to a better option. I also liked the idea of something humorous so it would create an effective pattern interrupt in my behavior. I was surfing the Internet one day looking for an appropriate response to this constant barrage of self-defeating chatter when I stumbled upon a video from the movie *Step Brothers* with Will Ferrell and John C. Reilly. By the end of the clip, I was laughing hysterically in my office and knew I had found my solution.

Will Ferrell's character Brennan is a nearly 40-year old, immature and unemployed leech who still lives with his mother. In the clip, he is meeting with a job placement specialist named Pam to explore his options. The only reason the meeting is taking place is because his new stepfather forced him to. As they introduce themselves, Brennan proceeds to carelessly butcher the specialist's name over and over with little regard for her emotional reaction. Meanwhile, she eventually notices that Brennan has brought his stepbrother Dale with him as well. Did I mention that they are both wearing tuxedos for a job that would require him to take out the trash? They proceed to continuously say her name wrong as Pam gets exceedingly frustrated with them. As she expresses this to them, they promptly tell her, "Shut your mouth." They continue to repeat this over and over again as she tries to talk. Eventually she has enough of their shenanigans and screams at them, "GET OUT-T-T-T-T OF MY OFFICE!"

Honestly, I can't really do this scene justice. It's really too ridiculous to capture it in words. I mean, who actually goes to an interview in a tuxedo with their stepbrother and then proceeds to tell the interviewee to shut up? It's all completely outrageous because Brennan and Dale are completely outrageous. I quickly realized that these two dudes were the exact type of characters I needed to get rid of my idiotic "inner roommate." I decided that every time I noticed my negative inner chatter starting to get going, I would simply imagine it in Brennan's voice. I knew that I would never be able to take the voice seriously ever again and this would create a powerful pattern interrupt. I found myself smiling every single time I heard my "inner roommate" Brennan telling me I should take it easy and draw back on my expectations. I wasn't going to take advice from this dude ever again!

Even though I found this a little amusing, I knew it didn't make sense to allow my "inner roommate" to hang around anymore. I had better things to be focusing on that would make my life much more dynamic and meaningful. So I decided it was time to channel my inner Pam. I flipped the script on Brennan by starting to tell him to "shut his mouth" every time he tried to chime in. Then I took things up a notch and ended the conversations for good. Rather than engage in them at all, I proceeded to tell Brennan that it was time for him to "GET OUT-T-T-T-T!" He had overstayed his welcome by an abundance of years and it was officially time for him to move on with his life.

Listen, I know this might sound pretty rude depending on your geography and/or background. If I'm being straight with you, never in a million years would I seriously say this to someone in real life. But honestly, nobody has also ever consistently talked to me in the manner that my "inner roommate" does. In my mind, the disrespect here calls for an entirely different level of emotional intensity. Think about it. This roommate shows up every time you try to pursue your goals and tells you that you aren't enough. Over and over, it has convinced you to settle for average as it pointed out all your "flaws." In my mind, this is what this "inner roommate" deserved for treating you that way for so long. They are just fortunate we didn't go all Godfather on them.

THE "BE MORE LOVING TO YOURSELF" BREAKTHROUGH

Once I had kicked out my negative "inner roommate" for good, it was time to step up and give my brain a much better option. I knew that this was going to be a critical step if I was going to flip the script on my negative inner chatter once and for all. I was sick of all of the limiting self-talk so I committed myself to finding a new approach that would free me up completely to pursue my value visions all out moving forward. With some reflection, I eventually stumbled upon a perspective that led me to a brand new self-talk strategy that radically transformed the way I spoke to myself.

The most powerful seed thought came when I wondered to myself what advice I would give to someone else who was in my exact same situation.

What would I tell someone who I was coaching?

Better yet, what would I tell the people I love most in the world?

What advice would I give them if they were holding back because of fear or if they believed they were not enough?

How would I show up for them daily to help them breakthrough in their life?

It only took me a second to recognize that I was not being fair to myself because I wasn't giving myself the same advice. I then had a profound realization.

I wasn't really giving myself advice or encouragement at all when it came to the barriers I was facing in my journey. Instead, I had allowed a negative "inner roommate" to talk me down from pursuing my aspirations all out the last couple of years.

Here is the honest truth. I would do anything in my power to help my wife and our kids realize their dreams. If they expressed a concern that they might not be enough to reach them, I would passionately reiterate the fact that they were incredible and had everything they needed to achieve their goals. If I sensed that fears were holding them up, I would tell them over and over to value growth and to love the process. I would express to them passionately and repeatedly that I love them unconditionally and believe in them with all my heart. I would flat out go out of my way to show them different ways that they were special and capable every single day until they saw it in themselves. It would be my number one mission in life to help them realize that they would always be more than enough.

As I reflected on my passionate responses to these profound questions, it became crystal clear that I was not doing any of these same things for myself. It didn't take me long reflecting on my coaching experiences to realize that this was a common trend in our society. I think it's safe to say that most of us are willing to show up and fight for the people we love, but we aren't always willing to do the same for ourselves. We will patiently listen to our closest friends' perceived inadequacies and immediately tell them with care and confidence that their beliefs are unwarranted because they are incredible people. When they tell us about their fear of falling short, we reassure them that they have what it takes to make their goals happen. The point is that if you are a good friend, you will always tell people you care about most that they are more than enough to achieve their goals. This is how it should be, right?

Now we get to the part where profound change happened for me. The truth was that I wasn't giving myself the same grace. I wasn't showing up and providing myself with the same advice that I would give my wife and kids. If I'm being honest, I had not once given myself the same empowering advice with conviction. Instead, I had been subtly reminding myself of the times when I had fallen short of expectations and allowed it to pull me back from pursuing my passion and purpose all out. I understand that this came from the

189

part of my reptilian brain that wanted to keep me safe, but that still didn't make it right. Not if I knew the difference and had a choice to see it differently. And not if I would passionately tell my closest friends and clients not to allow a little fear to stop them from pursuing their highest aspirations. It was time to take these insights and apply them into my own life.

I was in the middle of a meditation session one day when this exact thought process I am describing floated into my mind.

Why is it that I don't treat myself the same way I treat the people I love the most?

I knew I cared about myself, but I wasn't as intentionally supportive to myself as I was to others. I didn't really have an answer to this question.

Why don't I give myself the same advice in this exact moment that I would give to my kids if they were holding back on pursuing their dreams?

Again, I wasn't quite sure why I hadn't done this at any point in my journey. To be fair, I guess I had never even considered this as an option. Maybe this was the reason I hadn't done it. I knew that it was definitely an option now so there was no excuse not to step up and encourage and empower myself.

I didn't plan for this to happen, but my brain just sort of transitioned into a coaching role. I guess it sensed that it was time to treat myself with authenticity to the process that I believed in to my core. It was in the middle of this meditation session that I started to give myself the same advice I would give to my wife and kids.

I won't give up on you Coyte.

I love you too much to do that. I refuse to allow fear to stop you from launching a career you are passionate about.

I won't stand by and allow a few disappointments to keep you from living your purpose. You have everything you need right now to go out and make your dreams happen.

I will show up every single day and remind you that you will always be more than enough. God made you uniquely to do this exact thing. So stop holding back and go live all out doing what you are meant to be doing. You deserve to breakthrough in your life!

A tear trickled down the left side of my face in the middle of this session. A second one proceed to run down my right cheek as I realized that I had never really talked to myself in this way. Sure, I had done the "pump it up" self-talk to get myself amped up as an athlete. But it was much different than the way I was talking to myself now. This was far more encouraging and heartfelt. This was more like the advice that a loving parent would give their child in a time of struggle. I had honestly never talked to myself in a raw, self-loving manner that cut through my biggest barriers. It was a transformative moment for me because it made me fully realize that I was more than enough to go get the life I desire.

WHY IT SEEMS SO WEIRD

I started to wonder why I had never done this type of self-talk before. I immediately came to the conclusion that it honestly seems pretty weird to do it. Wouldn't you agree that most people think individuals who talk to themselves are a tad strange? In the movies, they might even characterize this type of behavior as insanity. Yet the fascinating thing is that my most profound thoughts and breakthroughs during this journey came when I was having an engaged conversation with myself. The other reason why I likely hadn't done it is because the idea of self-love is often seen as soft and fluffy in our society. Many people perceive it as a sign of weakness to need to talk to yourself in this manner. This is especially true when you are a male who grows up in a society that has generally taught you to "not complain" and "just tough it out." The problem is that this approach just flat out doesn't work when it comes to emotions.

Let's pump the brakes on these beliefs because they just don't hold up when you examine them. First off, most of us are already having subconscious conversations with ourselves all day long. The thing is that these are often negative and self-deflating. So often we are telling ourselves reasons why we aren't enough and why we can't achieve the outcomes we desire. With this being the case, we might as well throw the "it's weird to engage in self-talk" idea out the window because that ship has sailed.

Now on to the negative self-talk. To me, it seems far more strange to sit back and allow this dialogue to take place. Why would we ever consciously allow this to happen if we know the consequences? The answer is that we shouldn't. We wouldn't knowingly allow this to go on with the people we love most and we deserve the same type of respect.

When you take all of this into consideration, it seems like talking to yourself in a loving, supportive manner makes a whole lot of sense. If it is still considered strange, then call me the weirdest dude on the planet. I would rather be seen as odd while being kind, supportive and encouraging to myself than be seen as "normal" and uncaring, critical and discouraging to myself! Call me soft if that's what it means to love myself unconditionally. It's important to remind yourself that you are going to need real support if you are going to flip the script on your biggest remaining barriers and live to your potential. Might as well make a decision right now that will ensure that you always have what you need to create the life you desire. Besides, we already know that being a little odd is a requirement for going out and living a life that makes the world a cooler place.

SPEAK LIFE INTO YOUR OWN LIFE

I was finishing up a short warm-up routine when my wife Brandy joined me in our workout area. "Can you download a new song to our workout playlist?" she politely asked. "It's a really good song. I think you will like it." I nodded my head and promptly headed to Apple Music to search for it. I typed in *Speak Life* by TobyMac and it appeared on the screen. After it finished downloading on my phone, I pulled it to the top of our workout list and hit the play button. It was officially time to start our workout so I did a few stretches as I listened to the song playing on our Beats Pill. The words instantly grabbed my attention as they were totally relevant to my current "be more loving" emphasis.

Some days life feels perfect

Other days, it just ain't workin'

The good, the bad, the right, the wrong

And everything in between

Yo it's crazy, amazing

We can turn our heart through the words we say

Mountains crumble with every syllable

Hope can live or die

So speak life, speak life

To the deadest darkest night

Speak life, speak life

When the sun won't shine and you don't know why

Look into the eyes of the broken hearted

Watch them come alive as soon as you speak hope

You speak love, you speak

You speak li-i-i-i-i-ife, oh oh oh oh oh

You speak li-i-i-i-i-ife, oh oh oh oh oh.

I realized that the song was totally true. I believe it in my soul that this is totally possible if you are bold enough to intentionally speak into people's lives with passion. This is one of the reasons I had walked away from academia to pursue my dream of becoming an author, coach and speaker. In each of these roles, you have the opportunity to give people hope because you can choose to believe in them in ways that they don't necessarily believe in themselves yet. You can speak life into them by showing them ways to close the gap on the results and life they desire. All of this can be done while speaking continual words of encouragement that allows them to pull out their potential.

It is truly a magical thing to be able to step into someone else's life and help them believe they are capable of more. There was something in this song that made me want to push to do it even more and better in my life. It inspired me to believe that I was capable of doing it at a much higher level on a much broader scale. I decided that it made sense to make the *Speak Life* Motivantra a more prominent emphasis in my daily approach to living so I immediately inserted it into the end of my morning growth routine before I started writing this book. At first, I started by simply urging myself to *Speak Life* in my writing. I reminded myself of the incredible opportunity I had in front of me to inspire people to live to their highest potential. I told myself that I was blessed to be able to speak hope, to speak love and to speak LI-I-I-I-IFE into people's lives.

Then I got even more creative with my approach. I started to listen to the song after meditation and naturally started to move around my office. This quickly turned into dancing and before long I was moving dynamically and wildly throughout my whole downstairs area. This charged me up as I could vividly imagine the song playing at one of my future events as I inspired people to speak life into their own lives. I realized that this became another way of speaking life into my own life because this visualization reminded my brain that I was enough to go get my goals. It created an intense emotional response in my body that would carry over into my writing. I realized that I was much better when I was in a passionate state before doing my work.

I continued to flood my brain with the mantra to reinforce it. I figured that it made sense to add some reminders to hold myself accountable. I put *Speak Life* in a prominent position on our bathroom mirror in a nice fluorescent pink color. It was a reminder to speak words of encouragement and inspiration into my wife and kids' lives as I started my day. This was super helpful so I decided to do the same thing in my workspace. I would remind myself to do this every time I sat down to work on content for my new courses and coaching program. The end result of this simple shift was content that was far more raw, intentional and impactful. Within a few weeks of making this shift, I had received some of the best feedback I had ever received about my work.

It didn't take me long to realize that there was still one place in my life where I needed to implement this *Speak Life* Motivantra. I'm guessing you already know where I am going here. I was now doing a really solid job of speaking words of inspiration into the people's lives around me, but I was not consistently doing the same to myself. I knew I needed to be completely authentic in my new approach by giving myself the same gift. I committed to making this happen. At least once a day, I would stop and remind myself to speak life into my own life. The natural spot came during my morning dance routine in a part of the song that always fired me up. I would use this surge in ENERGY to remind myself that I had everything that I needed to pursue the life I was passionate about.

I know it may still sound a little strange to speak to yourself this way, but I hope you can get past the initial weirdness. Because in the middle of this activity is a powerful shift waiting to happen in your life. You see, sometimes all we need to breakthrough in our lives is for someone to believe in us. Stop waiting for someone to magically come along and do that for you. Instead, step up and embrace the initial awkwardness. Write down all the reasons why you are enough and have what it takes to close the gap on the life you desire. If you can't find it yet, write down what you would tell the most important person or people in your life if they were in your position. Then turn around and use this script on yourself. Look yourself in the mirror and tell yourself that you have everything you need to achieve your goals and dreams. Then keep showing up and following through on this activity until you believe it to your core.

YOU BELONG UP HERE

When Ron stepped into my life that day at Welsh Ryan Arena when I was 14-years old, he taught me the power of speaking life into another person's life. In an instant, he helped me realize that I was capable of so much more as an athlete and human being. This was a profound moment because it gave me the seed thought for understanding the unlimited power of beliefs and the mind. At the time, I honestly thought I was there to get experience, but Ron showed me that I actually belonged up with the best wrestlers in the country. This is a proud moment that I still carry with me to this day.

Now I want to channel my inner Ron and pass this powerful lesson on to you. I'll bring my best effort and hope that it's enough to speak life into your life. You are capable of extraordinary in your life. I hope you realize that. The fact that you are still reading and implementing these concepts means you are now a .000001 percent person because you are one of the few willing to actually fight to EARN change in your life. Pat yourself on the back for that. It's not easy to flip the script on barriers that are crazy common in our society and you have differentiated yourself as a human being. You are now ready to roll out remarkable and memorable in your life.

But these are a few small caveats.

Only if you start to speak to yourself in a manner that will pull out your highest potential.

Only if you learn to start having the encouraging types of conversations with yourself that you would have with loved ones who are pursuing their dreams.

Only if you find new ways to inspire yourself on a consistent daily basis to go get the goals that have been evading you in the past.

And only if you commit to taking action that allows you to believe in yourself unconditionally moving forward.

Here's the thing. This isn't unreasonable at all. It isn't out of your reach. It really just requires that you show up and invest in yourself. Honestly, it's something every person on the planet should be doing for themselves anyways. No matter what is going on around you, you should be willing to show up and speak life into your life every single day. Why?

Because you can.

Because you deserve it.

Because if you don't believe in yourself completely, it's more than possible that the people around you will not.

Because your ability to bring your own unique gifts out into the world depends on it.

I honestly didn't know how to make this happen when I started this journey. I had experienced a series of bigger disappointments in a 5-10 year period that were painful. These had caused me to question whether I was enough to actually go get the big dreams I now had for my life. I had some pretty lofty aspirations so I didn't have too many people around me who had the capacity to tell me I was capable of achieving my goals. Then I realized that it wasn't their job to do this anyways.

It was my job to step up and *Speak Life* into my dreams every single day.

It was my job to remind myself each morning that I was more than enough to create the life I desired.

It was my job to love myself unconditionally so I was willing to put myself out there and be all right with whatever criticism came with the territory.

FLIPPIN SELF-DEFEATING INNER CHATTER

Nobody really wants an inner voice to be the reason that they are not able to live to potential in their lives. It can be disappointing to realize that you are responsible for the biggest limiting barriers that are present in your life.

Rather than dwell on time lost, our job right now is to focus on the opportunity you currently have in front of you. It's entirely possible to dispose of your unwelcome "inner roommate" and replace it with a kind, supportive voice that speaks life into your own life. It's time to make all the self-defeating chatter flippin disappear once and for all. In its place, we can program a belief system that empowers you and pulls out your highest potential.

YELLOW BALL #10

THE "SPEAK LIFE" HABIT

We aren't going to reinvent the wheel here. You already have the foundation for this activity outlined in the chapter. So, let's keep it simple. It's time to speak life into your own life. But first we have some housekeeping to take care of.

Find a ridiculous character that you would never believe in a million years. This can be someone from a movie or real life that you can't take seriously.

Once you have this person in mind, pay attention to the negative chatter going on in your head as you move through your day. The moment you notice it, immediately pretend that it's coming from the ridiculous character you have chosen. I think you will find that it changes the way you see the situation entirely. Proceed to tell them to "shut their mouth"(or whatever version of this command you prefer) and tell them that it's time to get out so you can create space for a new empowering voice.

The final step is to determine exactly what you would tell someone you love with all your heart if they were in your exact situation right now with barriers stopping them from living to potential. Take some time to write out the heartfelt advice you would give them to help them break through and close the gap on their goals. Once you feel good about this, get up and start embracing your inner weird by striving to STAND OUT in your approach. How? I think you know! Just *Speak Life* into your own life every single morning even if it feels strange at first. Do it with proactive passion so you feel it and start to free your potential up.

And if that negative chatter happens to pop up again during your days, simply kick the "inner roommate" out again and redirect back to your empowering *Speak Life* speech points. Rinse and repeat this process until your norm is to inspire yourself to live to your highest potential.

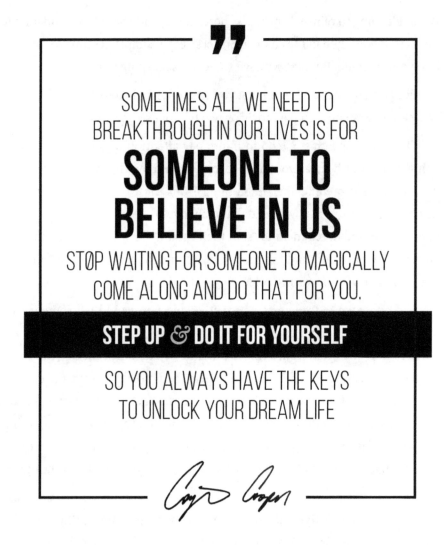

SOMETIMES ALL WE NEED TO
BREAKTHROUGH IN OUR LIVES IS FOR

SOMEONE TO
BELIEVE IN US

STØP WAITING FOR SOMEONE TO MAGICALLY
COME ALONG AND DO THAT FOR YOU.

STEP UP & DO IT FOR YOURSELF

SO YOU ALWAYS HAVE THE KEYS
TO UNLOCK YOUR DREAM LIFE

CONCLUSION:
THE FINAL FLIP
MAKE FEAR DISAPPEAR

"When you choose to perceive love over fear, life begins to flow."
—Gabrielle Bernstein

It was a sunny Friday morning in the Pacific Northwest as I sat down to write this final chapter. I honestly felt like I had everything I now needed to go get my desired outcomes and dream life. I had done the work to flip the script on my biggest barriers by giving my brain powerful new options that had radically increased my efficiency and quality of life. It was time to get out and really make things happen now. I was ready for a big breakthrough. There was only one problem. I still felt tension when it came to freeing up and taking the action necessary to close the gap on my goals. I was hesitating and holding back. After some thoughtful reflection, I realized that I still had one big barrier left to flip if I was going to live to my highest potential.

In hindsight, I should have recognized this obstacle sooner than I did. In traveling around the country, I had asked audiences over and over what the biggest barrier was that was stopping them from achieving their desired outcomes in life. Whether they were 16 or 78, corporate or non-profit, grieving or going after their goals, it always came down to one profound barrier:

FEAR.

I was blown away when the remarkable repetition of this response made me realize that this was the one universal barrier facing most people regardless of their backgrounds, demographics and/or preferences. I'm not sure why I would have ever assumed that I would be immune from this trend.

To be fair, this is not always something that is easy to diagnose. I now realize that the reason why it was so tricky for me to spot is because our brains are remarkably clever. They often don't give us a straight-forward "flight response" in the pursuit of our aspirations because that would be too easy to pinpoint. Instead, our stealthy subconscious brain often delivers us emotions such as confusion, distraction, frustration or overwhelm to keep us from pursuing our aspirations.

It turns out that distraction is my mind's mechanism of choice when striving to keep me safe. Every time I got close to pursuing something all out that truly mattered to me, my brain would barrage me with all kinds of different options and pull me off track. To keep me on my toes, it would also sprinkle in confusion at times hoping I would hesitate and lose momentum. I have come to realize that it is very effective at doing this.

You might be asking yourself, *But why? Why would your brain want to keep you from achieving your goals?*

It's important to point out that this isn't your brain's objective at all. If it knew that pleasure was certain in your pursuit, it would cooperate fully and embrace every aspect of the experience. The issue is that your brain is wired to keep you safe and the way it often does this is by keeping track of past situations that were painful. *Hey, Coyte. Remember that one time you pursued your goals at UNC? Yea-h-h-h-h-h, let's not do that again.* It doesn't want you to experience hurt again so it finds creative ways to get you to back down from the pursuit of your dreams.

I quickly realized that this was exactly what was happening in my life. I was allowing past situations to dictate my future. It wasn't reasonable at all. I knew that I had now arrived at my final barrier. Just like in the movies, I had saved my biggest dragon for the dramatic closing scene. If I was going to free up and be the hero of my own script, I knew I was going to have to figure out how to make fear disappear once and for all in my life. If I could learn to flip it, I had a chance to free up and live the life I was meant to be living. This naturally led me to a thought-provoking question.

Is it possible to release the past situations that are causing these fears?

As I reflected, I realized that the main fears that were now holding me up had been learned. In my mind, if I had learned them, I was convinced I could unlearn them. Now it was time to figure out how.

THE MAGIC OF MEDITATION

I still distinctly remember the first time I tried to meditate. It was five years earlier when I headed to my living room to give it my first shot. I sat cross legged in a traditional meditation pose on our main carpet area and set my iPhone timer to 5-minutes. Then I proceeded to close my eyes and focus on my deep breathing pattern. I was ready to CRUSH my meditation session! *On a side note, I have since learned that you never actually CRUSH your meditation session. That is a counterproductive focal point for what you are trying to accomplish.*

Everything was going great for about 10-seconds when I heard a beeper go off on our microwave.

I wonder what and the heck that was.

I guess maybe it's noon already.

I wonder what Brandy is cooking for dinner.

Oh, damn it! Back to my breathing!

I was just settling back into my meditation routine when I noticed the sound of a plane traveling overhead.

Huh, I wonder where that plane is headed. Maybe somewhere real nice like Hawaii?

Dude, seriously!!! GET-T-T-T-T BACK TO BREATHING!!!

I finally cleared my mind and had a few moments of breakthrough where I was momentarily feeling proud of my progress. Feeling like it certainly must be time to finish up, I opened my eyes up to check my timer. It had to be in silent mode because it felt like it had been at least 10 minutes since I started. As I clicked the button to turn it on, I was stunned by what I saw.

ONE MINUTE, FORTY-ONE SECONDS!

How is that even possible?

My iPhone timer has to be broken!

Well, I committed to five minutes so I need to get back to my breathing.

I settled back into my routine when I realized that my legs were killing me. I tried to brush this off, but I found myself unable to ignore the pain. I made an executive decision to straighten my legs out so I could point my brain back to my controlled breathing pattern.

I wonder if LeBron James meditates before his games.

Seriously, Coyte!!! FOCUS. ON. BREATHING.

The timer eventually went off after what could have arguably been the longest five minutes of my life.

Despite my underwhelming performance, I kept showing up each day committed to mastering this new habit. Eventually my persistence paid off because I had a breakthrough after a few weeks. I was locked in on my breathing one day when all of my thoughts cleared out and I got lost in the experience. It was a magical, calming feeling, as I learned what it meant to be completely centered. I didn't realize it at the time, but I had just learned an essential skill set that would serve as the foundation for one of the biggest breakthroughs in my life five years later.

THE ROOT OF MY FEARS

It took me some serious reflection, but I finally realized that all of my hesitation stemmed back to fear. I was afraid to cut loose completely. It wasn't intentional, but my biggest pains from my past were still lying dormant inside me, creating a drag on my potential. It was these unresolved memories that were hanging around consistently triggering a fear response in my day-to-day living. My subconscious brain would use these as a reference point as it found ways to pull me away from pursuing my purpose and potential.

I eventually came to the realization that the past situations were not actually the problem. They were what they were. The issue was that I had not dealt with the situations in a productive manner. I had done everything in my power to push my emotions down as quickly as possible so I could move on with my life without anyone noticing my pain.

In hindsight, it doesn't surprise me one bit that this is the way I handled it. This is the way many of us have been taught to deal with our emotions in our society. I have found this to be especially true if you are a male. It ratchets up to an entirely different level when you are a competitive athlete in a sport like wrestling.

You're not hurt.

Get your butt back in there...you're fine.

Stop crying. Real men don't cry.

Tough it out.

Here's the problem. I had situations where I actually was hurt. I distinctly remember moments as a college wrestler when I was so disappointed that I felt the urge to cry. A few tears occasionally found their way down to my cheek bones in private situations, but I quickly wiped them away and urged myself to be tough.

Strong people don't cry, Coyte. Remember?

It was counterproductive belief systems like this one that made me feel like it was wrong to experience these types of emotions. So I did everything in my power to push them down as quickly and efficiently as possible. I became a master at distraction and convincing myself that I had moved on. *Poof.* Just like that, my emotions started to disappear.

Phew, thank goodness...I'm back to normal.

At least, that's what I thought. On the surface, it seemed like everything was all good in my life. A few months after my tenure decision, I was totally convinced that this was the case. What I didn't realize is that a trusty friend had started tracking me the moment I had been denied tenure. They had stealthily been following me around keeping track of every step and decision because they wanted to make sure I didn't get hurt anymore in the future.

All right, before this gets too weird, let me admit that I didn't actually have some creepy stalker. I am talking about my Amygdala here. You know, the part of our brain that keeps track of situations that hurt us so we can avoid them in the future. Well, while I was pushing down emotions and redirecting to positive, it was dutifully keeping track of all of it for future reference. I can just imagine the inner commentary from Mygy (my nickname for my Amygdala) as I moved through the process.

Fine, don't acknowledge this situation. I will. Somebody has to be the responsible grown-up and keep track so we don't keep repeating situations that hurt us.

Meanwhile, I was cruising along trying to pretend like nothing had happened to me. In the process, I was pushing my emotions down and trying to convince myself that everything was on track and going as planned. Each time someone asked me how I was doing, I had a pretty standard response.

Yeah, I'm doing well. Everything happens for a reason.

Honestly, this second statement actually did turn out to be true. But not until I had gotten things straightened out with my trusty friend Mygy. At the time, I was using statements like this as a mask so I didn't have to admit that I was hurt. While it seemed harmless, it turned out to be the trigger for my biggest barrier because it was a strategy that was unknowingly leading me right to the fears that were now blocking my progress.

While I moved forward to pursue my new dream, Mygy was traveling alongside reminding me, "Hey, cool it my friend. This didn't end so well the last time." Over and over again, my buddy found ways to distract and talk me down so I didn't put us in another situation where we would be dominated by disappointment.

I eventually realized exactly what my subconscious brain was trying to accomplish. This is when I started to connect the dots on the steps I needed to take to make fear disappear. It was time to get things straight with Mygy. I needed to start giving him the respect he deserved and own up to my past painful situations. I had a feeling that this was the only way that he wouldn't keep reminding me of them each time I stepped up to pursue a new dream. It was time to face my most hurtful memories, the ones that I knew would inevitably bring up feelings of disappointment and shame.

PAUSE FOR THE CAUSE

Before we move on to a process that made fear disappear and radically transformed all areas of my life, I want to pause for the cause to make an important point here. For a long time, I didn't want to think about my past hurts and disappointments. They didn't make me feel good, so I avoided them at all costs. This ultimately became the thing that stopped me from progressing and freeing up in my life.

I have learned that I am not alone here. Most people are generally terrified to face up to their past painful memories. This likely has to do with the fact that there is often shame associated with falling short of expectations in our society. Each time we revisit a past memory where we were rejected, we feel lesser, and this drains our hope and ENERGY. Rather than deal with it, the most convenient coping mechanism is often to bury it and hope you never have to experience it again.

It sometimes makes you feel better to know that you are not alone. Human beings all over the world suffer pain that weighs heavily on their lives. *While a certain level of pain is unavoidable in life, it does not have to define us. Instead, it's entirely possible to free up your highest potential and close the gap on your dream life if you are willing to face up to your past "demons".* It turns out that this is one of the secrets to magically making fear disappear.

I HEAR YOU, BUT IT'S TIME TO MOVE ON...

I had done enough reading and research to know that one of the keys to flipping the script on fear was learning to deal with your most painful memories. I needed to be able to pull them up and just sit with them. I sensed that this would come from cultivating the ability to acknowledge my emotions, but not actually act on them.

Does this make sense?

I'm honestly not sure it would have made complete sense to me before moving through this process. Let me try to explain this a little better. It means developing your ability to sit with your past pains and acknowledging the emotions associated with them. However, here's the kicker. You do it in a way where you simply notice and recognize them *without any judgment.* The second part of this past statement is the most important part. This is the key to a breakthrough because it means that you will no longer associate shame (or any other dreadful verdict) with past situations.

Well, it just so turns out that the longest 5-minutes of my life had prepared me for this exact moment. Those three weeks where I slogged through my meditation sessions had eventually allowed me to develop a wonderful habit.

What exactly was this transformational skill set?

The ability to notice thoughts, but not act on them.

This is what I learned from meditation. It taught me that thoughts are simply a part of being human. You can certainly quiet this clutter a great deal, but completely silencing your brain is unreasonable. It was a relief when I realized this because I knew that my meditation practice was working. I eventually learned that the key to effective sessions was to learn to notice thoughts, but to not judge and/or act on them. Instead, I simply redirected back to my breath and guided meditation focal points. It turns out that both of these skill sets were critical for eventually making fear disappear.

It was a cool January morning in the Pacific Northwest when I put these meditation skill sets to work. I had risen early at 4:30am and decided that I would kick off my morning growth routine with 30-minutes of meditation. I settled in on my couch and set my timer on my watch. I knew exactly what I would do in this self-guided meditation session. Just like the first time I practiced five years ago, I focused on deep breathing and got my body into a completely relaxed state.

Once I felt completely calm, I decided that it was time to pull up my UNC tenure decision. I immediately felt a rush of emotions rise up in my body as I pictured the moment when my chair had broken the news. Confusion and frustration were the first to arrive on the scene. Then, just as quickly as they arrived, anger emerged in a flash and stole the spotlight. Finally, I experienced the disappointment I had felt when I replayed the fact that I had fallen short of expectations. As I experienced these emotions, I allowed them to come up and sat with them.

I didn't label them as good or bad.

I didn't follow any of the negative thoughts that popped into my brain.

I didn't judge or act on any of the emotions.

Instead, I simply experienced them as they were without any critic or negative inner dialogue. I just noticed them as they were at the time. I was fully aware that they were in the past now. Do you know what this helped me realize?

I'm all right. I'm still here doing just fine. They can't hurt me anymore.

I no longer need to avoid them. I am capable of facing them.

Once I had acknowledged my emotions, I intuitively knew that it was time to move on. I sensed that it was time to use my new *Speak Life* strategy. I was sitting in complete silence when I whispered to myself, "I hear you, brain. I understand what you have been trying to tell me. The situation was hurtful and you wanted to make sure it didn't happen again. You just wanted to keep me safe. I get that now. But it's time to release this situation and move on."

It was an emotional session for me, but I came out of it immediately feeling lighter. It was as if I had cut the ties to a 25-pound kettlebell that had been dragging behind me for three years. I knew that this session had allowed me to start flipping the script on fear. How? Because I was able to revisit my past most painful memories without the emotions overwhelming me. There were no longer any feelings of shame and I was now able to revisit them with a sense of relief.

I had officially taken a big step to release my past pains and flip the script on fear.

I can't say for sure exactly what your process will look like, but I know this for sure.

You can't bury your most painful memories if you want to break free in your life.

If you keep pushing them down, fear will keep popping up at inopportune times to drag on your progress and potential. If you want to truly excel and free up to pursue your dream life, you need to find a way to face up to your pains and release them once and for all.

Once I finished this session, there was one additional step that allowed me to put a cap on my efforts. It was during a follow-up meditation session that I intentionally revisited these past memories and intentionally asked myself, "What was the gift in each situation?" It only took me a few seconds to recognize that each instance had led me to the exact point I was at in my life and I was grateful for that. They were truly incredible gifts. I then once again took the advice of Marie Kondo and gave thanks to my past experiences for the lessons they had taught me.

Thank you, UNC! For all the memories and for giving me the opportunity to learn lessons that have made my life even more special.

It was through this process that I was able to release past memories that had been triggering counterproductive flight responses in my life. It turns out that I did in fact want a flight response. Just not the one where I ran away from my dream life. Instead, I wanted one where I let go of past pains so my good friend Mygy could board a plane and take a much-needed vacation. It was officially time for my loyal, overworked buddy to get a much-needed break after working too much overtime the past three years.

AN UNEXPECTED GIFT...

A few days after my morning meditation sessions where I released my past pains, I was sitting at my desk reflecting on my journey. I acknowledged the fact that I felt so much lighter in my daily approach to living. I was no longer carrying around nearly as much unnecessary baggage that bogged down my brain. This allowed me to think far more clearly. As I peered out the window to admire the majesty of Mount Baker across the bay, my mind suddenly became completely calm. The entire world faded away as I was left with only myself. This was just enough space to bring me an emotional realization.

I really love the person who is left.

Never in my life had I ever had a thought like this. Yet here I was reminiscing on all the work I had done the past three years. I had failed so many times during the journey, but I kept getting back up to face the barriers in front of me. It was this persistence that had given me the chance to flip the script on my biggest obstacles. With each flip, I had broken through a prominent barrier that had previously limited my potential. Now that I had released some past painful moments triggering fear, I actually had the space to reflect on the entire process.

When you clear all the clutter, all the unnecessary barriers, it turns out that there is something left once it is all gone. I have read that this is the core of who you are as a human being. Some refer to this as your soul. *Minus all the fears, doubts and limiting beliefs, there is a person deep inside of you that you are meant to be.* It dawned on me that I had never been properly introduced to this version of myself because there had always been too much going on in my life. It was different now as I sat in a serene silence.

Well, it turns out that I really liked the person that was left after all the inner work I had done. There was *far* less ego. I had been truly humbled by my tenure decision in a way that forced me to consider what truly mattered in my life. It was the struggle that had allowed me to finally get to know myself better. I was fascinated how this changed the way I felt about the person that was left standing.

I admired this person for their courage.

I appreciated this person for their willingness to keep showing up.

I loved this person for never giving up and fighting to arrive at this place.

I didn't have it all figured out. Heck, I still had all kinds of imperfections. My wife Brandy could tell you all about them if you had a few spare minutes. The difference now is that I didn't let them stop me from having an appreciation for who I had become as a human being the last few years. Even better, I had learned to point my brain to positive enough that it felt far more natural to honor who I had become during my journey. It was this ability to embrace the process that taught me some valuable, much needed lessons.

I didn't have to be perfect to be proud.

I didn't need a title to tell me I was enough.

I didn't have to achieve "lots" to love myself.

I need to pause here and emphasize that this wasn't the norm for me. I had grown up chasing lofty goals from the time I was five years old. I was insanely competitive as a kid. With each championship that I garnered, I appreciated it for a brief moment, but always wanted more. I distinctly remember winning a state title my junior year and immediately being frustrated because I didn't win by enough. While everyone else who had won was off celebrating, I was busy beating myself up.

On top of this, I was always pushing for the next title. Here's the thing with that. When you keep striving to perform at a high-level, eventually you are going to be met with some real resistance. At some point, everyone falls short of expectations. It's an inevitable consequence when you are a human being. In the times when this happened to me (which happened a decent amount in college), I was *really* hard on myself. I always wrongly believed that I was a "failure" when I didn't achieve my goals. This inevitably made me feel like I wasn't enough.

I now realize that this "always need to win," achieve more mentality was a recipe for disappointment. It was the type of focus that was going to lead me straight to frustration in my life. Why? Because I always needed something outside of myself to prove that I was enough. This was a losing battle because the goals were never going to fill the void. As you now know, I needed to change my entire focus to arrive at an end destination that filled my life with happiness, joy and love.

I NEEDED IT...

All of this striving did serve a purpose, though. It led me straight on a path to this journey. It put me face-to-face with a "failure" that I couldn't ignore. I never set out to accomplish self-love at the start of my journey. I honestly just wanted to feel better and to be able to provide for my family. Yet in the middle of this initial unwanted scenario, I was forced into situations that taught me profound lessons that radically altered the way I saw every part of my life. It was these perspective shifts outlined in this book that finally made me so incredibly grateful for the challenges I had faced the past three years.

Maybe this was always the gift.

Far too often, we look at life's challenges and automatically see them as a burden. Our ego doesn't allow us to initially consider the fact that they might be exactly what we need at this point in our lives. Yet if you are willing to face up to the "pains" put in your path, it often leads you straight to unexpected rewards that are far more pleasurable than anything you could have previously imagined possible. *But*...only if you are willing to face up to your biggest barriers so you can flip them and pull out your potential.

Here is the honest truth. I didn't love who I was before my tenure decision. I thought I did, but I was completely wrong. I now realize I was too busy allowing my ego to run the show as I chased down outcomes that would give me outside praise and recognition. *I didn't know what I didn't know at the time.* The crazy thing is that I always had enough inside of me and all around me. I just needed to slow my life down and take the time to see it.

I don't think I would have ever done it, though. I would have stayed on the never-ending treadmill of pursuing accolades trying to prove I was enough. Fortunately, God tapped me on the shoulder and quietly whispered, "You are on the wrong path, Coyte. It's time for you to sit on the sidelines for a bit so you can figure it all out." So, no...I didn't actually hear a voice delivering me this message. It was more like a metaphorical two-by-four hitting me across the chest, because that is what I needed to get my brain's attention.

I got knocked down, but I eventually got back up. And as I did, the journey eventually made me realize that I needed this downtime in my life. You see, in the middle of it, I was given obstacles that I needed to learn to overcome so I could start becoming the person that I was meant to be. I now realize that this was the only way I was going to strip my ego away enough to see that love was the key to living a truly meaningful life.

LETTING GO AND LETTING LOVE GUIDE THE WAY...

I wish I could tell you that I was insightful and wise enough to chart this entire path on my own, but I flat out wasn't. None of this was ever planned out and on purpose. Instead, my biggest breakthroughs started to come when I stopped trying to control everything and started to pay attention to the signs all around me. I began to trust that the universe would provide me the lessons needed to find my way and make my Value Visions come to fruition. Low and behold, as I quieted the clutter inside my brain, I started to receive timely messages that made my final step to flip fear once and for all crystal clear.

I needed to let love guide my approach more moving forward.

In a way, this reminded me of the heart rock I had found for my wife on our anniversary as I emphasized it in my morning routine. I started to think that maybe I just needed to be more intentional about making this a central focal point in every part of my life. This is when I extended the focus beyond my morning routine and started to push to make love the most important emphasis in my Sacred Space time periods. I quickly realized that there were four areas of emphasis that radically elevated my life.

Loving myself for who I am right now...

Loving the family I am blessed to have...

Loving the gift I have to impact lives each day...

Loving the opportunity God has given me to live this life...

I grabbed onto these and made them a central focal point in my morning meditation. As I moved into key Sacred Space times in my day, I intentionally reminded myself to love the opportunity in front of me. *Bring the Bliss, Coyte!* In the times when I started to sense negativity and lower emotional states, I flipped the script by redirecting back to these four areas of emphasis. They were so powerful that I started to refer to them as my "Core Four Love Affirmations." These helped me be authentic in modeling them daily.

When I learned to start loving who I was as a human being, I no longer felt the insatiable urge to prove myself. Don't misunderstand this to mean a lack of motivation, because I still had a deep passion to go out and live to my highest potential. This wasn't about settling. I just didn't need external outcomes nearly as much for the wrong reasons. I loved who I was *right now,* but I was still going to use every minute of my days to embrace the opportunity I had been given to build a remarkable family and career that filled me with abundance and joy.

I also reminded myself consistently that I was blessed to be living the day right in front of me. And within each day, I urged myself to love the fact that I had gifts that would allow me to impact people's lives if I was intentional with my approach. *Not obligation, Coyte…OPPORTUNITY.* All of this started to add up so I was able to actively express my love for the life God had given me by showing up and living it the best I possibly could every single day.

What happened next blew me away. *Poof!* As love began to occupy a larger presence in my life, fear finally disappeared once and for all. This is when I realized that I always had the power to eliminate lower level emotional states in my life if I got really good at making love a central focus in my approach to living. If I was just disciplined about pursuing my "Core Four Love Affirmations" each day, then unproductive fear that didn't serve me would never have a place in my life.

Do you want to know the coolest thing? This was an outcome that I could always control.

It is always in my control to stop and love the person I am.

It is always in my control to love the gifts that I have been given in my family and career.

And it is always in my control to love the opportunity God has given me to live this life right now.

This meant I could always EARN a loving presence where unwanted fears never had a prominent place in my life. I knew that this would always be something worth fighting for.

MY FINAL CONFESSION

It was December of 2018 and I was at an event in Las Vegas where I was the featured speaker for a business association. I had just finished up my Flip the Script keynote talk when the CEO of the organization approached me. As he shook my hand, he looked directly at me and said, "I am so glad that you got denied tenure at UNC because now the world gets to hear your message." I immediately gave him a heartfelt thanks, as it was one of the kindest things that anybody had ever said to me after one of my talks. As I walked away to head to the airport to go home, I reflected on what he had said to me. I smiled while getting into my Uber and thought to myself, *me too.*

Do you want to know something interesting, though? As we finish off our time together, I want to make a confession. I didn't always believe this statement. Sure, if you asked me early on, I would have told you that I was glad it happened. That was my pride talking. The truth is that there was still a big chunk of me deep down that was bitter that it had happened *to me.* I honestly felt like a victim. I now realize that this part of me, the same one that wanted UNC to regret their decision, felt like I had been cheated out of something that was mine.

It's fascinating how time, reflection and growth can change how you see things. That is, *if you let it by intentionally getting back up and looking for the lesson.* Right now, as I finish this final chapter three years later, I believe I got exactly what I deserved and needed. I very much needed every part of this journey as I progressed through this book for specific reasons I now understand.

I needed it because I was too selfish.

I needed it because I was valuing the wrong things.

I needed it because faith had no prominent place in my life.

I needed it because I wasn't living near my highest potential.

Most of all, I needed it because I was on the wrong path. It wasn't necessarily bad, but it was a path that was never going to lead me to my purpose. I didn't know it at the time, but it was not what I was meant to be doing as a human being.

Fortunately, the deserved part wasn't all bad. I realize now that while I might have deserved to be denied tenure, I also deserved to be in a place where I was appreciated for what I brought to the table as a professional and human being. I deserved to be in a spot where I was using the gifts God had given me to make the world a cooler place. One where I woke up every single day and loved my life unconditionally.

I needed all of the challenges in this journey to make these things happen.

But most of all, I needed and deserved the tenure decision because I didn't love myself.

It wasn't even on my radar, and if it had been, I would have not been able to tell you authentically that I did. This journey took me to unexpected places and taught me unforeseen lessons that changed all of this. With each flip that I made, I got closer and closer to my true self. When all the clutter was gone, I loved myself in a way I could not have possibly understood just three years earlier.

IT'S YOUR FLIPPIN CHOICE...

There was one more reason I needed to be denied tenure.

We needed to be able to take this journey together.

Even as I wrote the book, I envisioned a reader just like you to come along and step with me. This thought inspired me tremendously as I consistently ran up against obstacles that slowed my progress. I don't think I could have done this by myself. In the end, it was the idea of a chance to engage in a transformational conversation that kept me showing up passionate to cultivate a transformational experience.

I strove to create a storyline that would keep you curiously reading. I hoped I had done enough to guide you through an innovative process with the potential to create meaningful change in your life. I wanted to practice what I preached by EARNING the right to teach you powerful strategies to flip the script on your biggest barriers in life. But do you know the one thing that inspired me most in the end?

I wanted to be able to tell you with authenticity that you are completely capable of creating a life you love unconditionally.

That is, IF you step up and start exercising your inner Viktor Frankl. I guess in a way it makes sense that we end pretty much where we started. Because at the center of it all is a power of choice that you can always exercise as a human being. Never neglect this power, because it is one of the greatest gifts you have been given by your creator.

You can always choose to grab on to one single habit that has the potential to flip the script on your most prominent negative patterns. With each day that you choose to follow through and fight for it, you can train your brain to focus sharply on what is possible in your life. No matter what happens, it is always within reach to give your brain an empowering option that pulls out your highest potential.

Flip negative noise. How? *By training your brain to focus on and love growth in your morning routine.*

Flip scarcity. How? *By consistently redirecting your mind to all the wonderful blessings that are always present around you.*

Flip not enough. How? *By creating a vision that captures your mind's full attention and inspires you to take uncomfortable action.*

Flip instant gratification. How? *By deciding that you are the type of human being that will always take the path to EARN your highest aspirations.*

Flip flawless. How? *By pursuing passion daily and embracing every step of the process as a beginner.*

Flip self-doubt. How? *By identifying the person you believe you are meant to be and making a firm decision to finally STAND OUT in your life.*

Flip obligation. How? *By reminding yourself you are blessed to get the opportunity to do the things you love daily.*

Flip not present. How? *By deciding to intentionally make moments in the areas of your life that matter to you most.*

Flip good, but not great. How? *By refusing to settle in your life and instead committing to bringing bliss to your Sacred Space time frames.*

Flip self-defeating chatter. How? *By kicking out your negative inner roommate and owning your ability to speak life into your own life.*

Flip fear. How? *By releasing past pains and barriers so you can learn to love unconditionally who you are as a human being.*

Believe it or not, you can *always* choose to love the ability you have to give your brain a better option. There are literally thousands of empowering focal points at any moment just waiting to be utilized. Even if you are currently in a tough spot, it's possible to grab onto one single habit that will train your brain to find positive, productive and eventually possible in your life. If this still seems improbable, then I simply urge you to be curious and commit to following through on one "Yellow Ball" habit in this book for 66-days. I promise you that you won't regret it.

You can *always* choose to love who you are as a human being. This might be the single most important choice you make in your life because it will free you up to live with purpose. No matter what has happened in your life, you can stop and appreciate the journey you have traveled and who you have become in the process. If that isn't possible, you can love the fact that you were created for a reason, and that alone is worth appreciation.

Finally, you can *always* love the fact that you have a creator that put you on this planet. You have been chosen to live a life that truly matters. Even when you are not sure if you believe in yourself, it's always possible to look at the beauty around you and consider the fact that it's incredible that you are here living right now. Then remind yourself that you have remarkable gifts inside you waiting to come out. If that still seems out of reach, then simply go back through the chapters and continue to flip your biggest barriers so you can eventually arrive at a special place in your life.

But in the end, it will *always* be your choice to make. I just hope I have done enough to convince you to cut loose and go for it.

Underneath your biggest barriers is a human being that is fully capable of creating your dream life. It's time to let that person out. Not just a little bit. A LOT a bit. As you move forward with your journey, be adamant about finding unique ways to Speak Life into your own life.

You were made remarkable.

There are gifts inside of you that are unique to you as a human being that will make the world a cooler place once you pull them out.

You were made for this exact moment.

No matter what has happened in the past, you have everything you need to excel moving forward regardless of your circumstances.

You were made enough.

It doesn't matter what anyone has told you in the past. You are more than enough to get the results and life you desire. You just have to step up and claim who you are as a human being.

It's your time, my friend. You get one life, so you might as well make it flippin remarkable and memorable.

Step up and *Flip the Script* on your biggest barriers so you can experience the bliss of being authentically you and living to your highest potential.

Sincerely,

"

UNDERNEATH YOUR BIGGEST BARRIERS
IS A HUMAN BEING THAT IS FULLY CAPABLE
OF CREATING YOUR DREAM LIFE.

IT'S TIME TO LET
THAT PERSON OUT

NOT JUST A LITTLE BIT. A LOT A BIT

AS YOU MOVE FORWARD WITH YOUR JOURNEY,
BE ADAMANT ABOUT FINDING UNIQUE WAYS
TO SPEAK LIFE INTO YOUR OWN LIFE.

AWKNOWLEDGMENTS

As I finish this book, I can't help but feel overwhelmed with gratitude for all the people who helped make it possible. It only makes sense to start with the one person who encouraged me to take the journey that led to this book. Brandy, I am so thankful that you encouraged me to "go for it" and supported me so much throughout the writing process. Listening to my ideas is a full-time job and you did it with patience and grace.

I would also like to thank my family for always being there for me. Carter and Mya, you constantly inspire me to be better and your wonderful spirits make each day far more special in our household. I would also like to express gratitude to my parents, Gene and Lisa, for supporting me throughout the years and always giving me unconditional love. A shout out is also in order for my brother Matt who has always been one of my closest friends. Appreciate you Tank!

Thank you to my editor Mark Facciani who challenged me throughout the process and helped me become a much better writer. I am truly grateful for it my friend! I would also like to give a special thanks to my graphic designer Vincent Vi for the wonderful job you did making this book so unique. You are uber talented!

I want to take a moment to thank the mentors who have poured into my life over the last 10 years. A special thanks in particular to my former coach Ron who taught me to believe that I was capable of more. I would also like to express my appreciation to my friend Ken Hubbard for being such a wonderful leader and for helping me start my spiritual journey in life. This was a critical step while writing this book.

There are also the mentors who I have never met personally, but their profound words have poured into my life and gave me a chance to live to my highest potential. A special shout out to Brendon Burchard, Brene Brown, Elizbeth Gilbert, John Maxwell, Lewis Howes, Oprah Winfrey, Rachel Hollis, Robin Sharma, Tony Robbins and Vishen Lakhiani for being wonderful guiding lights in the world. I am better because of the work you do in this world!

Finally, I just want to thank my partner in crime one last time. Brandy, never once did you ask me to give up on my dream during this journey. Not even when our bank account and savings were running low. You always believed in me and I am truly grateful for that! This book was only possible because you were always there loving and believing in me every step of the way!

ABOUT THE AUTHOR

Coyte Cooper, Ph.D. is a bestselling author, keynote speaker and executive coach who is one of the premier experts in the areas of personal leadership and maximizing human potential. A former NCAA Division I All-American, college professor, TEDx speaker and the current founder/CEO of Earn the Right (ETR) Coaching, Coyte has worked closely with thousands of proactive professionals the past few years to develop a unique transformational system that helps audience members radically enhance their clarity, focus, ENERGY, motivation, passion and results on a consistent daily basis. Coyte is a proud father of two and lives in Anacortes, Washington with his beautiful wife Brandy.

CONTACT COYTE

If you would like to share your "flip the script" success stories
with Coyte, you can write him at

coytecooper@ollinliving.com

This email can also be used if you are interested in learning more about
Coyte's coaching, speaking and training opportunities.

CPSIA information can be obtained
at www.ICGtesting.com
Printed in the USA
BVHW011923071019
560447BV00004B/18/P

9 780990 563648